A Song of My Spiritual Life

by Je Tsongkapa
with a commentary by
Choney Lama Drakpa Shedrup

translated by Gibson Chang
with Geshe Michael Roach

T0349039

Volume 123 of the Diamond Cutter Classics Series

Diamond Cutter Press
6490 Arizona Route 179A
Sedona, Arizona 86351 USA

ISBN 978-1-937114-53-4

Cover illustration by Jacques Cazo Seronde
Book design by Manolin Lorente & Rosa van Grieken

Table of Contents

Dedication

I dedicate the effort of this book to my parents, Mao Kuan Chang and Li Duan Liu, for their unconditional support; to my dear wife, Emily Chan, for exploring this exceptional wisdom together; to my first Tibetan language teacher, Word Smith, who keeps encouraging me; to Asian Legacy Library director John Brady, for patiently teaching me and giving me the chance to serve; and lastly to the guiding light of my life, the best friend of everyone, unbeknownst to them, Geshe Michael Roach.

—Gibson Chang

And I would like to dedicate these efforts to the two great teachers of my life: my dear wife Veronica, lifelong spiritual companion; and Khen Rinpoche Geshe Lobsang Tharchin, who first granted me the priceless teaching on the steps to the path.

—Geshe Michael Roach

Preface

Without exaggeration, we can say that the Tibetan master Je Tsongkapa (1357-1419) was the greatest Buddhist writer who ever lived in this world. There survive over 325 works, totaling more than 12,000 pages, of his writings on the huge range of every major topic of open & secret Buddhism. And when Je Tsongkapa[1] writes a single page, it contains a hundred pages of deep ideas, often expressed in sentences that require us normal people to pause for many minutes, to try to grasp all the detail & nuance he is expressing.

Je Tsongkapa was not just a writer; rather, he was the ultimate Buddhist practitioner as well. He personally mastered the myriad practices of classical Buddhism found in the almost 5,000 extraordinary books that survive from ancient India, the homeland of this religion, and there is no one before or since who has had a greater comprehension of their entire contents.

Your translators of this volume have had the honor of working, for over 10 years, on an extensive traditional biography of Je Tsongkapa, in over 400 pages, now published separately under the title of *King of the Dharma: The Illustrated Life of Je Tsongkapa*.

---

[1] *Je Tsongkapa:* This is, incidentally, the correct way to write our author's name in English pronunciation. Other ways of doing it are confusing transcription with pronunciation.

We encourage our readers to pick up a copy of the e-book or paper book and enjoy the detail, to appreciate his life fully.

The volume also includes some 150 different scenes from a traditional set of 15 color *tangkas* or scroll paintings of the Master's life, their final form dating from the early 1700's. It's exciting to get a peek at what actual people and settings in his story would have looked like.

In this more extensive biography, we were able to identify some 33 different roles that Je Rinpoche played in his life. This title, "Je Rinpoche," is by the way another popular name for Je Tsongkapa—who was also known by his ordination name, Lobsang Drakpa. The title "Je" means "Lord," and was used in ancient times for example in reference to a king, queen, princess or prince, or famed religious figure—male or female.

"Tsongkapa" literally means "the one from Tsongka," referring to a region in East Tibet which featured fields and a river named after the onions (*tsong*) that grew there—for this is where our author was born. "Rinpoche" means "Jewel," and is often added to the name of a respected spiritual figure.

Finally, "Lobsang" means "Pure Mind," and "Drakpa" means "Famous One"; especially in the sense of a person whose spiritual teachings have spread widely and helped many people.

The most remarkable thing about the slim volume you hold in your hands is this. In the many thousand pages of his priceless writings, Je Tsongkapa almost never speaks about himself. Only in the present work do we see the famous words—

> I, the deep practitioner,
> Have accomplished my practice
> This way;

> And you who hope for freedom
> Should do your practice
> The same.

Thus it is that the title of our brief work here is *A Song of My Spiritual Life;* or, in Tibetan, *Je Rinpochey Nyamgur.* "Je Rinpoche," again, literally means "Precious Lord." And *nyamgur* (technical spelling *nyams-mgur*) connotes a "song (*gur*) of personal religious experience (*nyam*)." In the West, the most well-known use of the word *gur* is in the title of the famous songs of spiritual experience written by the Tibetan meditator saint, Milarepa (traditionally dated 1040-1123AD). The name of his work has often been translated into English as *The Hundred Thousand Songs of Milarepa.*[2]

Another traditional name for our present work is *Lam Rim Dudun* (technical spelling *Lam-rim bsdus-don*), which translates as *The Briefer Presentation of the Steps of the Path to Enlightenment.* The work is also sometimes referred to as *Lam Rim Chung-ngu,* which means *The Smaller Book on the Steps.*

These titles serve to place the work in the context of several longer presentations on these steps composed by Je Tsongkapa, such as his massive *Great Book on the Steps to the Path* (*Lam Rim Chenmo*)— perhaps the most famous book ever written in the Tibetan language.

Although we have not located any specific mention of the date of the *Song's* composition, Je Tsongkapa himself mentions the location of his "headquarters" monastery of Ganden in the colophon, which would indicate that (as we might expect for a "song of personal experience") he wrote these lines about the steps of his path during the final decade of his life.

And just what are the "steps to the path"? These can perhaps best be summarized in terms of what the literature itself refers to as "people of the three capacities";

---

[2] *The Hundred Thousand Songs:* This is perhaps an overly-literal translation of the Tibetan word *bum* (technical spelling *'bum*), which does mean "hundred thousand," but traditionally simply refers to the *collected writings* of an author (as in *gsung-'bum*).

that is, practitioners of lesser capacity, practitioners of medium capacity, and those of greater capacity.

It's crucial to appreciate that we need to reach the level of a "practitioner of lesser capacity" just to *start* walking down the steps of the path. To start at this start, one thing is necessary: we have to show we are rational, by acknowledging the probability that we have past & future lives. That is, simply, anything that can happen once can very logically happen again, given infinite time or chances to do so.

If you throw a pair of dice once, then the odds of getting two "sixes" are, of course, somewhat limited. But if you throw the same pair of dice over time which may well be infinite, well then of course you will get two sixes an infinite number of times as well. We have been here, and we will come back here, infinite times.

The door just to start on the steps of the path is to acknowledge this undeniable truth; because the steps of the path for those of lesser capacity are meant to help us avoid going somewhere terrible after we die from this life. Therefore we can say that even reading the first page of this tiny volume is reserved for those who have enough self-honesty to admit the obvious: none of us will survive this life, and we need to "pack our bag" properly for the next one.

The practitioner of "medium" capacity is thinking on a bit larger scale. They acknowledge that it would be better, at minimum, to go after they die to a lifetime as a human somewhat similar to what they've had here. But then they look at all the pain and disappointment they've lived through this time, and the inevitable collapse of the healthy human body. They decide to set their sights on a future form which has no pain or trouble at all.

That is, if there have been periods (however brief) in this life when we were truly happy and reasonably healthy, then those periods must have had a cause. Again—being strictly logical, and not as a point of faith—it makes sense that if we could identify and re-create causes like this, then we could live a life which is uninterrupted and unmarred by any kind of suffering, ever again.

The practitioner of "greater" capacity is traditionally explained as a person who feels pain even more acutely than the lesser & medium. They are so sensitive to anything that hurts, that they automatically sense the pain, intimately, which other people around them are going through.

And so they share the same forward focus of the lesser & medium types: their goals *begin* with a good death, and travel to a good place, and a good place that is free of every single trouble of the place they are just about to leave: the rest of this present life.

But on top of this, they admit another logical certainty. If there are other people that we can see in this present world of ours, who are hurting, then given that the boundaries of space are (so far as we can now observe) beyond any limit—there must be in that infinite expanse of stars other worlds, where other beings not so different from us live, and suffer.

And again—logically—there is no rational reason why I would want to stop only the pain of other people whom I can see and touch in my own miniscule community, my own family or town. I may not hear, with my own ears, the cries of sick children in another country; but we can all hear those cries with the ears of our own logic: we know they must be there, which is to know they are there.

And once we hear them—even just with logic—then they are (says the person of greater capacity) as much my responsibility to help as my own daughter or son, lying in bed inside my own house. This then is why the person of greater capacity learns and carries out the steps of the path that you find—incredibly, in their entirety—within this tiny book.

In keeping with Je Rinpoche's intentions with this work, we will keep this introduction brief, and leave it at that; but it says everything. There are wondrous writings of almost infinitely more detail for you to enjoy, when you are ready to go deeper into the steps on the path. We highly recommend one of three full volumes in the English translation, entitled *A Gift of Liberation, Thrust Into the Palms of Our Hands.*

This masterpiece is a record of 24 days of incredible, detailed teaching delivered in Tibet in 1921, by Pabongka Rinpoche, Dechen Nyingpo (1878-1941). The transcript was taken (in a time before recording devices) by his disciple Kyabje Trijang Rinpoche (1901-1981), who then over many years' time carefully edited the record into what is certainly the greatest example of purely native Tibetan literature ever produced.

The greatest disciple of this teacher was in turn Khen Rinpoche Geshe Lobsang Tharchin (1921-2004), who with his own great disciple Dr. Artemus Engle (b. 1948) then produced the masterful English translation as *Liberation in Our Hands.* There are also available free videos online at *TheKnowledgeBase.com* of 14 years of lectures on this entire work by one of our present translators, Geshe Michael Roach.

It's extremely nice to have a real master introduce to us Je Tsongkapa's famous verses of the *Song of My Spiritual Life.* Of the many explanations of these lines, perhaps the greatest concise commentary has been composed by the wonderful Choney Lama, Drakpa Shedrup, who lived 1675-1748.

Choney Lama is a famed philosophical writer from East Tibet who also wrote amazing textbooks for the illustrious Sera Mey Monastic University in Lhasa, central Tibet. He is at the same time an extremely knowledgeable, accurate philosopher of the classics of Buddhism, and also an extremely accessible commentator with a decidedly Western style; he even once dreamed of flying—crosslegged—through the sky on his own power to "western lands" he had never really heard of, to spread the wisdom there.

For those who are interested, we have included a detailed biography of this sage in the introduction to our translation of the Diamond Cutter Sutra and Choney Lama's wonderful commentary to it (the clearest ever written). This translation may be found in the present Diamond Cutter Classics Series, under the title of *Sunlight on the Path to Freedom: A Commentary to the Diamond Cutter Sutra*.

Over 25 years ago, our team began translating—in addition to our collection of the massive, major classics of Buddhist philosophy—a series of "pocket books" meant to be carried in your purse or shoulder bag, as you walk around the world. We named this imprint the "Classics of Middle Asia Series," and we are happy to report that we've received many communications from people who had great insights into the steps on the path, just as they read a few pages in a bus or subway on their way to work.

And so we really encourage you to keep a copy of this little book with you as you pass through your day, and give it a glance whenever you have a few minutes. It will surely change your life.

Gibson Chang
Pondok Saraswati
Ubud, Bali

Geshe Michael Roach
Rainbow House
Rimrock, Arizona, USA
January 2025

Acknowledgements

Here at the Diamond Cutter Classics project, we often refer to the process of translating a new book as "snow on the mountain," meaning that the entire process of putting out a new work closely resembles the way in which snow falls upon a high mountain peak; gradually melts; and then wends its way down the mountain to the valleys—and from there inevitably to feed the ocean.

Our thanks to all the people whose hard work to make our translations possible follows the same pattern.

First, at the peak of the mountain, is the snow-treasure of the Asian Legacy Library's free online database of ancient Asian books. Millions of pages have been scanned or input in searchable form, under the leadership of executive director John Brady, over the last 35 years. He is assisted by—just to name a few—Emma Lewis, Christine Vimala Sperber, Christina Kasica, Joel Crawford, Arina Garcia, Osiris Luciano, Ben Ghalmi, Ven. Phil Baker, and Alona Stoliarchuk.

The massive labor of inputting all of the Tibetan works in the database over all of these years has been completed by the ALL Input Operator Team, headed now for many years by Ms. Sonam Lhamo. At the National Library of Mongolia, the catalog team has been led by the Library Director, Ms. Bayarkhuu Ichinkhorloo; and the Project Manager, Dr. Sainbileg Byambadorj. The new cataloging project at Gandantegchinlen Library is led by Ven. Munkhbaatar Batchuluun.

ALL's Sanskrit materials are input at the Varanasi

ALL Input Center, under the direction of Dr. Santosh Dwivedi; the Kathmandu ALL Input Center, directed by Drs. Miroj & Milan Shakya; and the Kerala ALL Input Center, directed by Dr. N.V. Ramachandran. Thank you all for your endless work!

We are very grateful for Aisha Nguyen, who tirelessly searches every corner of the web for any and all Sanskrit materials that we may need input; as well as David & Nancy Reigle, for helping to define and provide us with the most accurate, high-quality editions possible of any work in the Sanskrit language. We also thank Stanley Chen for his advice on Chinese-language sources, especially for the ancient crown of knives equivalent, its characters and drawing.

The cataloging and input work cannot be accessed without the priceless subject cataloging by the Diamond Cutter Classics team dedicated to this 35-year effort, now led by Nicholas Lashaw, Ben Kramer, and Geshe Michael Roach. Nick & Ben also manage the DCC translator team, including all our fellow translators, and we would like to share deep gratitude with every one of them—you keep us going!

We are also infinitely indebted to all those who support the work of Diamond Cutter Classics, around the world; including our tireless and deeply dedicated sponsors. We rely heavily upon the fine work of the Buddhist Digital Resource Center (BDRC) for obtaining original scans of the many source works our translations require. The Head Librarian, Karma Gongde, has offered us years of wonderful service and advice; and BDRC Executive Director Dr. Jann Ronis and Chief Technology Officer Élie Roux continue to give all of us really excellent support.

The next step in translation is the manuscript editing, which for technical books like this one is always a massive effort. We would especially like to thank Anatole Nguyen, Bets Greer, Nick Lashaw, and all the other editors contributing their time. We are in awe of the work by the Diamond Cutter Press staff, who get all these translations out into the world—especially in the new ebook formats, and dedicated DCP app. Thank you Rosa van Grieken, Ven. Elizabeth van der Pas, Katey Fetch, and master artist Gina Rivera. A very special thanks to Jacques Cazo Seronde for the beautiful cover illustration of Je Tsongkapa.

Our entire translation team would have no central place to meet and conduct the many hundreds of translation sessions that books like this require, without the offices in Sedona, Arizona, supplied through years of effort by John Brady; Connie O'Brien; Tim Lowenhaupt; and Gail Deutsch.

We are also extremely grateful for the special sponsorship of the entire Diamond Cutter Classics translation team. Recently, the expenses of our team have in addition been covered through the Good Night Book Club project, led by Lindsay Jilk and regional directors Inna Ivanina (Europe & North America); Tina Lyu (mainland China); Olga Van-Dick (Latin America); Nguyen Cong Binh (Vietnam); and Sugeng Shi & Xintian Ie (East & Southeast Asia).

Our grateful thanks to all of you, and to everyone else who has contributed to our work. Your trust in us is a big part of the reason why we can complete projects—like the present volume—which require quite nearly a decade each.

About the Translators

Gibson Chang

I'm one of the translators on the Diamond Cutter Classics team. Growing up helping out at my family's food stall, I witnessed my parents sacrificing their health to earn a living. I saw my grandparents arguing and complaining over trivial matters. These experiences led me to ponder: "Why do these things happen? What defines a truly meaningful life?"

In 2012, a friend recommended to me a business book called *The Diamond Cutter.* A concept in the book deeply fascinated me: "Your world comes from how you have treated others in the past." This was a viewpoint I had never heard before, which filled me with curiosity and made me eager to find the author, to unlock the questions in my heart.

When I found out that Geshe Michael Roach and the Diamond Cutter Institute Global (DCIG) team were coming to Taiwan to hold an offline program, I immediately signed up to volunteer and serve while I learned. By practicing the Four Steps, my relationship at home gradually improved, and I even met my partner, Emily. And then we learned, and served DCIG together.

Later, with the encouragement of a friend, Emily and I went to Mexico for our first "Steps on the Path" course. In class, I heard Geshe Michael Roach teaching this text from the original Tibetan. I vividly remember an indescribable sense of déjà vu welling up in me at the end of the first class, as if I had met this language and this wisdom somewhere before. It was at that moment that I made up my mind to learn the Tibetan language.

What made me determined to keep learning was the following sentence from Geshe Michael:

> Imagine that this ancient Asian classic in front of you is more precious than a cure for cancer; the wisdom within the classics can defeat death itself. And there are not just one, but hundreds of thousands of such classics. However, the people who can translate these books are extremely few—it's like a city of hundreds of thousands of people, with only one or two doctors available to treat them.

When the Diamond Cutter Translation project was launched in 2017, I applied to attend the on-site program of the Mixed Nuts translation group in Sedona, USA, three times a year. I started as an auditor and fully immersed myself in learning, studying how to translate Tibetan classics into language that modern people can understand and apply to their daily lives.

At the end of one translation session, Geshe Michael said to the translators, "If you want to improve your translation skills, a very important seed is to support the preservation of the ancient classics of Asia."

From then on, I began to help ALL (Asian Legacy Library) in preserving texts and raising funds. I also visited the National Library of Mongolia with John Brady, where I witnessed how ALL staff painstakingly scanned these texts and uploaded them to the internet for scholars and translators to use, free of charge. Holding these ancient books, which were written by masters 400-500 years ago, in my hands, I was filled with pure respect, and my determination to pursue my mission of translation grew even stronger.

Being invited by Geshe Michael to jointly translate this book, *Song of my Spiritual Life*, is of great significance to me, as this was exactly the content I first heard Geshe

Michael teach in Mexico many years before. Moreover, the author Je Tsongkapa also happened to answer a question I had over a decade ago:

> And spend every hour
> of the day & night
> working to get the very essence
> out of it.

In hindsight, I think I was very lucky. From the very beginning, when I was introduced to DCIG, learning the story of The Pen; and then on to further study of the Path; and now to dedicate myself to the translation of the classics—this journey is like living at the foot of a mountain, and at first only drinking from clear water flowing down from the snowy peaks, but ultimately finding the source of the spring and beginning to participate in the preservation, translation, and teaching of precious classics from the source: helping people use this wisdom to improve their lives, and create a better world.

I am deeply grateful to Geshe Michael for inspiring my passion for ancient wisdom and the original languages. I feel deeply honored to have the opportunity to help more people benefit from this precious, timeless wisdom.

Geshe Michael Roach

Michael Roach was born in Los Angeles and grew up in Phoenix, Arizona. He graduated with honors from Princeton University, and is a recipient of the Presidential Scholar medallion from the President of the United States at the White House. He has also received the McConnell Scholarship Prize from the Princeton School of Public & International Affairs, as well as an honorary doctorate in the Congress of Mexico from the National Autonomous University of Mexico (UNAM).

Michael is the first foreigner in the 600-year history of Tibet's Sera Mey Monastery to receive the title of Geshe (Master of Buddhism), after 25 years of study. After graduation, he founded the Asian Classics Institute (ACI), translating over 20,000 pages of the geshe course and designing 36 courses of studies in English, for modern people of all walks of life.

At his teacher's directive, Michael—in order to confirm that the principles of the ancient texts could be used in modern life—helped in 1981 to found the Andin International Corporation, which became one of the largest diamond jewelry companies in the world, and was purchased by super-investor Warren Buffett in 2009. Michael used the majority of his income from the business to found and run the Asian Classics Input Project (now called ALL, or Asian Legacy Library), starting in 1987. This is the largest free, online searchable database of ancient Asian literature in the world.

Michael also helped found the Three Jewels Outreach Center of New York; DCI Global; the Sedona College of International Management; the Yoga Studies Institute; Green Stretch Pen; Diamond Mountain Retreat Center; The Knowledge Base; Diamond Cutter Press; DSEU University; Classics Soft Power; Innovation Retreats; and the Diamond Cutter Classics translation center.

Each of these institutions helps preserve and make available the precious wisdom of ancient Asia, in the modern world.

Michael is the author of some 100 books and major translations. His most popular works include *The Diamond Cutter: The Buddha on Managing Your Business & Your Life;* and *How Yoga Works.* He lives in the small town of Rimrock, Arizona, with his wife Veronica, whom he first met some 50 years ago. Together they enjoy gardening, charitable work, yoga & gym trips, and running their small Peach Tree Café, for local cowboys & cowgirls.

A Song of My Spiritual Life
Je Tsongkapa

[1]
[f. 1a]
*,,LAM RIM BSDUS DON GYI TSIG 'GREL SNYING PO MDOR BSDUS
GSAL BA ZHES BYA BA BZHUGS SO,,

Herein contained is *A Brief Clarification of the Heart: A
Word-by-Word Commentary to "An Abbreviated Presentation
of the Steps to the Path."*[3]

[2]
,[f. 1b] NA MO SU MA TI K'I TI {%RTA} YE,

Namo Sumati Kirtaye:
I bow down to Sumati Kirti.[4]

[3]
,THUGS BSKYED MGYOGS 'GRO'I SHUGS KYIS NYER DRANGS PA'I,
,GZHAN PHAN 'PHRIN LAS 'GRO BA'I DPAL DU SHAR,
,SKAL LDAN PADMO YONGS KYI GNYEN GCIG PO,
,THUB DBANG SMRA BA'I NYI MA DE LA 'DUD,

You are drawn forth

---

[3] *Abbreviated Presentation of the Steps to the Path:* Please see the preface to
this volume for more information about the title.
[4] *Sumati Kirti:* This is the Sanskrit version of Je Tsongkapa's ordination
name, which is "Lobsang Drakpa," or "Pure-Minded One of Great
Renown"; in the technical Tibetan, *Blo-bzang grags-pa.* The technical
Sanskrit spelling is *Sumati Kīrti.*

By the power of
The swift ones of the Wish;

You rise in the sky
In a glory of holy deeds
That help all other beings.

You are the one friend
Of all the lotus blooms
Who have sufficient goodness;

And I bow down
To the Lord of the Able,
Sun among all teachers.

[4]
,BLO CHEN GZHAN GYIS SHIN TU DPAG DKA' BA'I,
,ZAB DON LEGS PAR 'GREL BA'I RNAM DPYOD KYIS,
,BZANG PO'I MDZAD MCHOG GRAGS PA'I SNANG BA CAN,
,RJE BTZUN BLA MA'I ZHABS LA GUS PHYAG 'TSAL,

With the excellent insight
Of your incredible *mind*,

You offered extraordinary
Commentary upon the profound—

Something that others
Found difficult to fathom.

Your *purest* deeds
Shone forth, with light
Above all, and *known to all*.

I bow down then,
In deep respect,
At the precious feet

Of my high & holy Lama.[5]

[5]
,GANG DE'I LEGS PAR BSHAD PA'I MTHAR THUG NI,
,BYANG CHUB LAM GYI RIM PA ZHES GRAGS PA,
,DE YI GNAD KUN GCIG TU RAB BSGRIL PA,
,LAM RIM BSDUS PA'I DGONGS DON GSAL BAR BYA,

> The ultimate example
> Of all the fine words
> Of explanation that
> He ever gave
>
> Is the famous
> "Steps on the path
> To enlightenment";
>
> And his *Abbreviated Presentation*
> *Of the Steps to the Path*
> Is one in which
> He perfectly combined
>
> All of its crucial points
> In but a single place.
>
> I will clarify here then
> The true intent of his work.

[6]
,DE LA 'DIR BDAG CAG GI BLA MA CHOS KYI RGYAL PO BTZONG
KHA PA CHEN POS MDZAD PA'I NYAMS MGUR RAM, LAM RIM
BSDUS PA'I DON NI GANG BSHAD PAR BYA BA'I CHOS SO,,

---

[5] *High & holy Lama:* In a common classical Tibetan literary device, the parts of a high lama's name are tucked into a verse of poetry. We have italicized these parts for the reader; in Tibetan, a small "x" mark would typically be carved under them.

What then is the work that we are going to explain in this commentary? It will be *A Song of My Spiritual Life*, which is also known as *An Abbreviated Presentation of the Steps to the Path*. This was composed by our Lama, the King of the Dharma, the great Tsongkapa.

[7]
'DI LA GSUM, SNGON 'GRO MCHOD BRJOD SOGS DANG, DNGOS GZHI GZHUNG DON DANG, MJUG GI BSHAD PA'I KHYAD PAR RO,,

Our explanation will proceed in three parts: the preliminary steps such as the offering of praise and so forth; the meaning of the actual text of the work; and then details of the closing section of the composition.

[8]
DANG PO LA GNYIS, MCHOD PAR BRJOD PA DANG, BSHAD BYA NGOS BZUNG BA'O,,

The first of these parts has two sections of its own: the offering of praise, and an identification of what it is we will be explaining.

[9]

[opening prostration]
NA MO GU RU MANYDZU GHO sh'A YA,
Namo Guru Manjughoshaya.

I bow down to my Teacher, Gentle Voice.

[10]
DANG PO LA'ANG GNYIS TE, DANG PO NI, LA LAR NA MO GU RU MANYDZU GHO sh'A YA, ZHES 'BYUNG BA NI SLA'O,,

The first of these sections also has two divisions of its own.

As for the first, the opening prostration that we see in some editions of the work—*Namo Guru Manjughoshaya*—is easily understood.[6]

Bowing to the Lord of the Able Ones

[11]
GNYIS PA LA LNGA LAS, DANG PO THUB DBANG LA PHYAG 'TSAL BA NI, ,PHUN TSOGS DGE LEGS BYE BAS BSKRUN PA'I SKU, ,ZHES SOGS RKANG PA BZHI STE,

The second division here has five parts of its own. The first is bowing down to the Lord of the Able Ones. This is expressed in the four lines [of the Tibetan] which begin with "Your holy body was produced by billions of perfect good deeds."

[12]

(1)

`,,PHUN TSOGS DGE LEGS BYE BAS BSKRUN PA'I SKU,
,MTHA' YAS 'GRO BA'I RE BA SKONG BA'I GSUNG,
,MA LUS SHES BYA JI BZHIN GZIGS PA'I THUGS,
,SH'AKYA'I GTZO BO DE LA MGOS PHYAG 'TSAL,

**Your holy body
Was birthed by**

**Billions of perfect
Good deeds;**

Your holy words

---

[6] *Namo Guru Manjughoshaya:* Which is to say, "I bow down to my Teacher, Manjushri"—the Buddha of Wisdom, whose name means "Gentle Voice." The point is that emptiness constantly whispers its truth to us.

Fulfil the hopes
Of infinite living beings;

Your holy mind
Sees all things
In the universe
Exactly as they are;

I touch my head
To the feet
Of that leader
Of the Shakya clan.

[13]
'DI LA MKHYEN BRTZE NUS GSUM MAM, SPANGS RTOGS KYI YON
TAN SPYI DANG, BYE BRAG **SKU**'I YON TAN GYI DBANG DU BYAS
NA,

We can consider these lines in terms of the three famous
qualities of knowledge, love, and power; or according
to the general division of good qualities into those that
relate to giving up certain things, and realizing others;
or relative, more specifically, to fine qualities of the *holy
body.*

[14]
MTSAN DANG DPE BYAD SOGS [f. 2a] YON TAN DU MAS KHYAD
PAR DU BYAS PA DE NI, RGYU GANG LAS 'KHRUNGS PA YOD DE,

When we distinguish Lord Buddha in terms of his
possession of many fine qualities relating to the signs &
marks of an Enlightened Being and the like, we can first
point to the cause that has produced these features.

[15]
BSOD NAMS DANG YE SHES KYIS BSDUS PA **PHUN** SUM **TSOGS**
PA'I **DGE LEGS** RE RE TZAM MA YIN PAR **BYE BAS BSKRUN PA** STE
BSKYED PA YIN PA'I PHYIR RO,,

And that's because the features have each been *"birthed,"* or created, not by just single examples of absolutely *perfect good deeds,* but rather *by billions* of them.

[16]
'DIR BYE BA ZHES PA NI, MANG TSIG YIN GYI, GRANGS KYI BYE BA TZAM LA MI BZUNG NGO,,

And when we say "billions" here, it's only meant to convey a great number; you shouldn't consider it in this case as a specific number.

[17]
MTSAN DPE RE RE LA RGYU JI TZAM DGOS PA NI, RIN CHEN 'PHRENG BA LAS GSAL LA, RGYU SO SO BA RE RE'I DBANG DU BYAS PA NI, YUM GYI MDO SOGS DANG, MNGON RTOGS RGYAN NA'ANG YOD DO,,

Just what kinds of causes are required for each one of the signs & marks of an Enlightened Being? This is generally clarified in *The String of Precious Jewels;* but if you would like to get into more detail on the causes behind each of them, that may be found in the Mother Sutras and the like—as well as in the *Jewel of Realizations.*[7]

[18]
GSUNG GI YON TAN LA NGO BO'I DBANG DU BYAS NA'ANG RUNG LA 'BRAS BU'I DBANG DU BYAS NA,

---

[7] *Causes for the signs & marks:* For the reference in the *String of Precious Jewels* of Arya Nagarjuna (c. 200AD), see f. 113b (entry S2 in the attached bibliography of works originally written in Sanskrit, corresponding to catalog number TD04158 of the Derge edition of the Tengyur, or collection of classical Indian Buddhist commentaries).

There are multiple references in the Mother Sutras spoken by Lord Buddha himself (500BC); see for example the description starting at f. 335a in the third part of *The Perfection of Wisdom in 25,000 Lines* (S5, KL00009-3).

For the description in the *Jewel of Realizations* of Lord Maitreya and Arya Asanga (c. 350AD), see the section starting at f. 11b (S3, TD03786).

Now we could just as well describe the fine qualities of the speech of the Buddha according to their essential nature; but let's look at them according to the effect that they inspire.

[19]
DE BZHIN GSHEGS PA'I **GSUNG** GI YON TAN NAM BYED LAS YOD DE, GRANGS **MTHA' YAS** PA'I **'GRO BA'I** GNAS SKABS DANG MTHAR THUG GI **RE BA SKONG BA**R BYED PA'I PHYIR RO,,

Now there is a certain fine quality or function of the *holy words* of One Gone Thus; which is that it serves to *fulfil* both *the* immediate and ultimate *hopes of living beings* who are *infinite* in number.

[20]
RE BA SKONG TSUL YANG, CHOS BSTAN NAS MNGON MTHO DANG NGES LEGS LA BKOD PA'I SGO NAS PHAN 'DOGS PA DANG, DE DANG DE'I SKABS KYI THE TSOM GCOD PA LA BYA'O,,

And just how does it fulfil these hopes? The Buddhas first teach the Dharma, which then places living beings in the attainment of the higher births and definite good.[8] This is how they benefit these beings, and remove their doubts at each different point in their development.

[21]
THUGS KYI YON TAN GYI KHYAD PAR YOD DE, NGO BO'I DBANG DU BYAS NA **MA LUS** JI LTA JI SNYED KYI **SHES BYA** THAMS CAD **JI BZHIN** MNGON SUM DU **GZIGS PA'I** PHYIR RO,,

Which brings us to the fine qualities of the *holy mind* of the Buddha. Relative to its basic nature, this mind *sees*—directly—*all things in the universe,* both in terms of the way they are, and the total number there are: the total

---

[8] *Definite good:* A code word for nirvana & enlightenment.

quantity, *exactly as they are.*

[22]
DE LTA BU'I SKU GSUNG THUGS KYI YON TAN DANG LDAN PA,
SH'AKYA'I RIGS KYI **GTZO BO** SH'AKYA THUB PA **DE LA** JI LTAR
PHYAG 'TSAL BA YOD DE,

And then finally there is a way that we bow down *to that*
Shakyamuni—to the *leader of the Shakya clan* or people
who possesses the fine qualities of holy body, speech,
and mind that we've described here.

[23]
YAN LAG GI DAM PA **MGO** BOS **PHYAG 'TSAL** BA STE 'DUD PAR
BYED PA'I PHYIR RO,,

And this is that *I* bow myself down, bend and touch *my
head*—the highest part of our body—*to his feet.*

Bowing to Loving One & Gentle Voice

[24]
GNYIS PA NI, ZLA MED STON PA DE YI, ZHES SOGS BZHI STE,
PHYAG 'TSAL LO,,

Which brings us to the second of our five parts here. This
is the *bowing down* found in the four lines [of the Tibetan]
which include "...of the matchless Teacher":

[25]
(2)
,ZLA MED STON PA DE YI SRAS KYI MCHOG
,RGYAL BA'I MDZAD PA KUN GYI KHUR BSNAMS NAS,
,GRANGS MED ZHING DU SPRUL PAS RNAM ROL BA,
,MI PHAM 'JAM PA'I DBYANGS LA PHYAG 'TSAL LO,

**I bow down to
The Undefeatable,**

And to Gentle Voice:

**The two highest children
Of the matchless Teacher,**

**Who took upon themselves
The heavy load
Of all the Victor's deeds,
Engaging in the divine play
With emanations sent
To countless different realms.**

[26]
GANG LA NA, 'GRAN **ZLA MED** PA'I **STON PA DE YI** CHOS KYI **SRAS** BYANG SEMS RNAMS **KYI** NANG NAS **MCHOG** [f. 2b] TU GYUR CING **RGYAL BA** DE'I SKU GSUNG THUGS KYI **MDZAD PA KUN GYI KHUR BSNAMS** PA STE BZHES **NAS**

And just who is it that we prostrate to here? There are certain Dharma *children of the matchless Teacher*—the one who is beyond compare. And there are *two* among them who are *highest,* and *who took upon themselves the heavy load of all the* holy *deeds* of this *Victor;* that is, two who agreed to carry out the actions that he performs in his holy body, and speech, and thought.

[27]
'JIG RTEN GYI KHAMS 'DIR MA ZAD **GRANGS MED** PA'I SANGS RGYAS KYI **ZHING DU** BYANG SEMS SOGS **SPRUL PA** DU MA'I GAR GYIS **RNAM** PAR **ROL BA** CAN **MI PHAM** BYAMS PA DANG '**JAM PA'I DBYANGS** GNYIS LA'O,,

And these are *"The Undefeatable"*—a reference to Loving One, Maitreya—*and Gentle Voice,* Manjushri. They are *engaging in* their *divine play* not only in the world of this particular planet, but also in a dance *with* many different *emanations*—as bodhisattvas and the like—*sent to countless different,* enlightened *realms.* I bow then to both of them.

[28]
MDZAD PA'I KHUR BZHES TSUL NI, BYAMS 'JAM DBYANGS GNYIS
KYIS THUB PA'I DAM PA'I CHOS SPYI DANG, KHYAD PAR RGYA
CHEN SPYOD PA DANG ZAB MO'I LTA BA'I BRGYUD RIM BZUNG
STE SPEL BAR MDZAD PA 'DI'O,,

And just how do they "take upon themselves the
heavy load of the deeds"? This consists of the two of
Loving One and Gentle Voice upholding, or we can say
furthering, the holy Dharma of the Able One in general;
as well as—most especially—the combination of the
generations of the lineages of widespread activities, and
profound view.[9]

Bowing to the innovators

[29]
GSUM PA NI, SHIN TU DPAG PAR DKA' BA SOGS BZHI STE, **PHYAG
'TSAL LO,,**

Which brings us to our third part from above—where *"I
prostrate"* in the four lines [in the Tibetan] that include
"extremely difficult to fathom":

[30]

(3)
,SHIN TU DPAG PAR DKA' BA RGYAL BA'I YUM,
,JI BZHIN DGONGS PA 'GREL MDZAD 'DZAM GLING RGYAN,
,KLU SGRUB THOGS MED CES NI SA GSUM NA,
,YONGS SU GRAGS PA'I ZHABS LA BDAG PHYAG 'TSAL,

---

[9] *Widespread activities & profound view:* "Widespread activities" is a
term used for the activities of a bodhisattva—a person seeking to help
every being in the wide, wide universe. "Profound view" refers to the
understanding of emptiness which facilitates these activities.

I prostrate
At the holy feet
Of those known
As Nagarjuna & Asanga,

So widely famed
Through the three realms.

You are true jewels
Of our world
Who undertook
To comment,

In a perfectly
Accurate way,

Upon the true thought
Of the Mother Sutras
Of the Victors,

So extremely difficult
To fathom.

[31]
GANG LA NA, RGYAL BA'I GSUNG RAB SPYI DANG KHYAD PAR, **SHIN TU DPAG PAR** TE RTOGS PAR **DKA' BA RGYAL BA'I YUM** RGYAS 'BRING BSDUS PA GSUM GYI DON JI LTA BA **BZHIN** DU **DGONGS PA 'GREL** PAR **MDZAD** PA'I SGO NAS **'DZAM GLING** GI **RGYAN** DU GYUR PA

And just who is it that we bow to, in these lines? There are masters *who undertook to comment, in a perfectly accurate way, upon the true thought* of that highest of the spoken word, that of the victorious Buddha. More specifically, they explained *the* three *Mother Sutras of the Victors*—the more detailed, medium, and briefer versions, which are *so extremely difficult to "fathom"*: to grasp. And by doing all this, they became *true jewels of our world.*

[32]
MTSON LA MGON PO **KLU SGRUB** DANG 'PHAGS PA **THOGS MED CES NI** SA 'OG SA STENG SA BLA STE **SA GSUM NA YONGS SU GRAGS PA'I ZHABS LA**'O,,

To represent the entire group of these jewels,[10] we have here *"those known as Nagarjuna & Arya Asanga."* And then our author is prostrating *at the holy feet* of these sages, *so widely famed through* the entire world of *the three realms* — which here refers to below the surface of the earth; upon it; and above it.

[33]
GANG GIS NA, DE {% **BDAG**} BLO BZANG GRAGS PA'I DPAL GYIS SO,,

And who, finally, is it that performs this prostration? It is *"I"* — a reference to the glorious Tsongkapa, Lobsang Drakpa.

Bowing to Lord Atisha

[34]
BZHI PA NI, SHING RTA CHEN PO GNYIS LAS SOGS BZHI STE, '**DUD DO**,,

Next comes the fourth part from above, where our author *bows down* again in the four lines [in the Tibetan] which

---

[10] *Entire group of the jewels:* This group is traditionally listed as six, with some variations between lists. A typical version would include the two "jewels of the middle way," Arya Nagarjuna (c. 200AD) and his heart disciple, Master Aryadeva (c. 250AD); the two "jewels of higher knowledge," Arya Asanga and his half-brother, Master Vasubandhu (c. 350AD); and the two "jewels of accurate perception," Masters Dignaga (c. 440AD) and Dharmakirti (c. 650AD). This way of listing the six is from the *Great Dictionary* (B16, R00002); see the entry under *rGyan drug* in any of the various editions.

include "from the two great innovators."

[35]

(4)

,SHING RTA CHEN PO GNYIS LAS LEGS BRGYUD PA'I,
,ZAB MO'I LTA BA RGYA CHEN SPYOD PA'I LAM,
,MA NOR YONGS SU RDZOGS PA'I GNAD BSDUS PA'I,
,GDAMS PA'I MDZOD 'DZIN MAR ME MDZAD LA 'DUD,

I bow down to
Dipankara,
Maker of Lamps,

Who holds a great treasure
Of advices which incorporate,
Unerringly,

Each & every one of
The essential points

Of the paths
Of the profound view
And widespread activities

Descended so perfectly
From the two
Great innovators.

[36]

GANG LA NA, **SHING RTA CHEN PO** KLU SGRUB DANG THOGS
MED RNAM PA **GNYIS LAS LEGS** PAR **BRGYUD PA'I ZAB MO
LTA BA** DANG, **RGYA CHEN SPYOD PA'I LAM** GYI RIM PA TSANG
LA **MA NOR** BAR **YONGS SU RDZOGS PA'I GNAD BSDUS PA'I
GDAMS PA'I MDZOD 'DZIN** PA DPAL **MAR ME MDZAD** LA'O,,

Who then does our author bow to, in these lines? It is
Dipankara, "Maker of Lamps," which is the glorious Lord
Atisha. This is because he is a *holder of a great treasure
of advices which incorporate each & every one of the essential*

points of the steps of the way — completely, and *unerringly*. And these are the *paths of the profound view, and widespread activities*, which have *descended so perfectly from the two great innovators*: Arya Nagarjuna, and Arya Asanga.

[37]
DE YANG JO BO CHEN POS BLA MA GSER GLING PA BSTEN NAS BYAMS PA DANG THOGS MED NAS BRGYUD PA'I GDAMS PA GSAN LA, RIGS {%RIG} PA'I KHU BYUG BSTEN NAS 'JAM DBYANGS DANG KLU SGRUB NAS BRGYUD PA'I GANG SA DUD {%BRGYUD PA'I GDAMS PA} MA LUS PA GSAN NAS GDAMS PA'I CHU BO GNYIS ZUNG DU 'BREL BAR MDZAD DO,,

Now the Great Lord learned the advices that came down through Loving One and Asanga by studying with the Lama of the Golden Isle. And he learned all the advices that descended through Gentle Voice and Arya Nagarjuna by studying with the master Vidya Kokila. And then he undertook to combine the flows of these two teaching traditions.[11]

Bowing to spiritual friends

[38]
LNGA PA NI, RAB 'BYAMS GSUNG RAB KUN LA SOGS BZHI STE, **PHYAG 'TSAL LO,,**

Which brings us to our fifth and final part from before;

---

[11] *Two teaching traditions:* "Lama of the Golden Isle" is a reference to Suvarna Dvipa Guru, whose personal name was Dharmakirti, not to be confused with the later master of logic and perceptual theory by the same name. He lived on the island of Sumatra c. 1000AD; a presentation about his life, and that of his contemporaries, may be found in the preface to the Diamond Cutter Classics publication *Deathless Nectar for Helping Others: Notes to a Teaching on the "Crown of Knives"* (bibliography entry E2 below). Vidya Kokila, an Indian master of the Middle Way school, is also dated to about 1000AD. It seems that his name should be correctly spelled in Tibetan as *Rig-pa'i khu-byug,* rather than *Rigs-pa'i khu-byug.*

this covers the phrase *"I bow down"* as found in the verse of four lines [in the Tibetan] which include "all the high teachings."

[39]

(5)

,RAB 'BYAMS GSUNG RAB KUN LA LTA BA'I MIG
,SKAL BZANG THAR PAR BGROD PA'I 'JUG NGOGS MCHOG
,BRTZE BAS BSKYOD PA'I THABS MKHAS MDZAD PA YIS,
,GSAL MDZAD BSHES GNYEN RNAMS LA GUS PHYAG 'TSAL,

I bow down
To all those spiritual friends
Who utilize a variety
Of skillful means

To clarify these teachings,
Moved by their love.

They are eyes to view
All of the myriad forms
Of high teachings—

The very highest
Point of entry for those
Of sufficient goodness
To make the journey
To freedom.

[40]
GANG LA NA, PHYOGS RE TZAM MA YIN PAR **RAB 'BYAMS GSUNG RAB KUN LA LTA BA'I MIG** TU GYUR CING, **SKAL** BA **BZANG** POR GYUR PA'I GDUL BYA **THAR PAR BGROD PA'I 'JUG NGOGS** TE LAM [f. 3a] **MCHOG** TU GYUR PA'I SKYES BU GSUM GYI LAM GYI RIM PA 'DI NYID, **BRTZE BA**'I THUGS KYIS **BSKYOD PA** STE DRANGS PA'I **THABS MKHAS** KYI **MDZAD PA YIS** GDUL BYA LA **GSAL** BAR **MDZAD** PA'I **BSHES GNYEN** RNAMS LA'O,,

And who is it that we bow down to in this verse? It is

42

to all of those spiritual friends who utilize a variety of skillful means to clarify these teachings to their disciples, "*moved by*"—compelled by—*their* heart's *love.*

And what are those teachings? They are these very steps on the path, which themselves constitute *the very highest* of all paths for individuals of three different capacities. These steps serve as *eyes to view* the content of *all*—and not just individual pieces—*of the myriad forms of high teachings.* And they serve as well as an *entry point* for disciples of *sufficient goodness to make the journey to freedom.*

[41]
TSUL JI LTAR NA, TSIG TZAM MA YIN PAR YID **GUS** PA'I SGO NAS SO,,

And in what way do we bow down to these holy beings? We do so not just in our words; but rather in great respect, mentally.

[42]
'DIR LTA BA'I MIG CES PA NI, KHA CIG BSHES GNYEN LA SBYOR BAR SNANG YANG, LAM RIM NYID LA BYED PAR RJE'I DGONGS PA YIN PAR LAM RIM CHEN MO'I MJUG TU GSAL LO,,

When we speak here of "eyes to view," it would appear that some people hold that the phrase applies to the spiritual friends mentioned. It's clear though from the concluding section of *The Great Book on the Steps of the Path* that it was meant by Lord Tsongkapa to refer to the teaching on the steps of the path, itself.[12]

---

[12] *Concluding section of the "Great Book":* Je Rinpoche does indeed speak specifically to this topic in the final piece of one of his longest & most famous classics. See the section at f. 519a beginning from *Thub-pa'i gsung-rab rab-'byams* (B8, S05392L).

A jewel and the sun

[43]
GNYIS PA BSHAD BYA NGOS BZUNG BA LA GSUM, BRGYUD PA'I
KHYAD PAR, KHYAD CHOS, DGOS PA'O,,

This brings us to our second larger section from above—
an identification of what it is we will be explaining. This
we cover in three parts: a feature of the lineage; specific
other features; and the purpose.

[44]
DANG PO NI, 'DZAM GLING MKHAS PA YONGS KYI SOGS BZHI
STE,

The first of these is found in the four lines [of the Tibetan]
which include "all the masters of this world."

[45]

(6)

,'DZAM GLING MKHAS PA YONGS KYI GTZUG GI RGYAN,
,SNYAN PA'I BA DAN 'GRO NA LHANG NGE BA,
,KLU SGRUB THOGS MED GNYIS LAS RIM BZHIN DU,
,LEGS BRGYUD BYANG CHUB LAM GYI RIM PA NI,

The steps on the path
To enlightenment,

Passed down
With such excellence,
In their own stages,
Through the two
Of Nagarjuna and Asanga,

Are a jewel on the topknot
Of each & every master
Upon this planet;

A victory banner
Of great renown,
Glorious here
Among beings.

[46]
'DZAM GLING 'DIR BYON PA'I **MKHAS PA YONGS KYI GTZUG
GI RGYAN** DU GYUR CING, MKHAS PA'I **SNYAN PA** PHYOGS KUN
DU GRAGS PA'I **BA DAN 'GRO** BA'I GNAS 'DI NA NYI MA LTAR
LHANG NGER GSAL **BA KLU SGRUB** DANG **THOGS MED GNYIS
LAS RIM PA BZHIN DU LEGS** PAR BRGYUD PA'I **BYANG CHUB
LAM GYI RIM PA**'I GZHUNG NYID 'CHAD PAR BYA'O,,

The steps on the path to enlightenment—as they have been
*passed down with such excellence, in their own stages, through
the two of Nagarjuna and Asanga*—are like the *jewel on the
topknot* upon the heads of *each & every master* who has
ever come to *this planet*. They shine in *glory here* in the
world of *beings* like the sun itself, upon the peak where
we see flying the *victory banner of* the *great renown* of these
masters, waving proudly in fame that reaches every
direction. And it is a classic work upon these steps that
"I will now explain to you."

[47]
ZHES RTZOM PA DAM BCA' DON GYIS MDZAD DO,,

In this section then our author has, by implication,
expressed the traditional commitment to compose the
work.

Metaphors for the steps

[48]
GNYIS PA LA GNYIS, DPE DON GYI KHYAD PAR DANG, KHYAD
CHOS DNGOS SO,,

With this then we have reached our second part, on the specific other features. This comes in two sections: specific metaphors and their intent, and then the actual features.

[49]

DANG PO NI, SKYE RGU'I 'DOD DON MA LUS SKONG BAS NA, ,SOGS BZHI STE,

The first of these is expressed in the four lines [of the Tibetan] which include "for they fulfil each & every one of the aspirations of beings."

[50]

(7)
,SKYE DGU'I 'DOD DON MA LUS SKONG BAS NA,
,GDAMS PA RIN CHEN DBANG GI RGYAL PO STE,
,GZHUNG BZANG STONG GI CHU BO 'DU BA'I PHYIR,
,DPAL LDAN LEGS PAR BSHAD PA'I RGYA MTSO'ANG YIN,

> These are an instruction
> Which is the very king
> Among the lords
> Of all jewels,
>
> For they fulfil
> Each & every one of the
> Aspirations of beings.
>
> They combine the rivers
> Of a thousand
> Beautiful classics;
>
> As such, they are
> A glorious ocean
> Of fine explanation.

[51]
DE LTAR BRGYUD PA'I BYANG CHUB LAM GYI RIM PA 'DI NI, DPE
DON GYI KHYAD PAR JI LTA BU DANG LDAN ZHE NA,

One may begin here by asking, "You have described then
steps of the path to enlightenment that have come down
through a certain lineage; are there any metaphors, and
their intent, which apply here?"

[52]
YOD DE, THAR 'DOD KYI **SKYE RGU'I 'DOD DON MA LUS** PA
SKONG BAS NA, GDAMS PA RIN CHEN DBANG GI RGYAL PO
LTA BU **STE,** YID BZHIN GYI NOR BU RIN PO CHE DANG CHOS
MTSUNGS SHING,

In fact, there are. *These* teachings on the steps to the path
are an instruction which is like *the very king among the lords
of all jewels; for they fulfil each & every one of the aspirations
of* those *beings* who seek for freedom. Which is to say,
these teachings are just the same as that gem we refer to
as a "wishing jewel."[13]

[53]
THEG PA CHE CHUNG GI **GZHUNG** LUGS **BZANG** PO **STONG GI**
LEGS BSHAD KYI **CHU BO** MA LUS PA **'DU BA'I PHYIR** NA, **DPAL
LDAN** TE PHUN SUM TSOGS PA **LEGS PAR BSHAD PA'I RGYA
MTSO** LTA BU'**ANG YIN** NO,,

The teachings on the steps, further, *combine* all *the rivers
of* fine explanation that we find in *a thousand beautiful*
systems of *classic* texts within both the greater and
the lesser ways.[14] *As such they are* very much like *a*

---

[13] *Wishing jewel:* The ancient Asian equivalent of an Aladdin's Lamp, this
is a common gemstone found in a river; treated with sacred substances;
and then prayed over at the top of a staff, on a special holy day—which
imparts the power to grant its owner anything they wish for.
[14] *Greater and lesser ways:* The "greater way" is spiritual practice
motivated by an intention to serve, eventually, every living being in the
universe. The "lesser way" is motivated, for the time being, by a desire

"glorious"—which is to say, absolutely perfect—*ocean of fine explanation.*

[54]
'DOD PA'I DON SKANG TSUL NI, 'DI'I DON NYAMS SU BLANGS PA LAS MNGON MTHO DANG NGES LEGS 'GRUB PA DANG,

And how is it that the steps fulfil wishes? If we put into actual practice the ideas that the steps teach us, then we achieve higher rebirths, and definite good.

[55]
GZHUNG LUGS STONG STE MANG TSIG SMOS PA YIN PAS GRANGS STONG KHO NAR MI BZUNG ZHING,

When the root text here refers to "a thousand beautiful classics," you should understand that this is simply a large number that was chosen; in actuality, these great works are hardly limited to only a thousand.

[56]
DE RNAMS 'DU TSUL YANG RJOD BYED KYI TSIG THAMS CAD 'DU BA'I DON MIN GYI [f. 3b] BRJOD BYA'I DON MTHA' DAG 'DU BA'O,,

And when we say that the steps "combine" all of these works, it doesn't mean to say that they include the total amount of their specific wording. Rather, the steps include all of the actual content that these works embody.

---

to avoid a bad rebirth, and all the sufferings of a normal life. The second leads, in time, to the first.

Features of the steps

[57]
GNYIS PA NI, BSTAN PA THAMS CAD 'GAL MED SOGS BZHI STE,

Which brings us to our second topic here: the specific features of the steps. This point is covered in the four lines [of the Tibetan] which include "Each one of the teachings is completely compatible with all the others."

[58]

(8)
,BSTAN PA THAMS CAD 'GAL MED RTOGS
PA DANG,
,GSUNG RAB MA LUS GDAMS PAR 'CHAR BA DANG,
,RGYAL BA'I DGONGS PA BDE BLAG RNYED [f. 56a] PA DANG,
,NYES SPYOD CHEN PO'I G-YANG SA LAS KYANG BSRUNG,

The steps also allow us
To grasp that each one
Of the teachings

Is completely compatible
With all the others.

They also make it possible
For all the classic teachings
Of the Buddha to strike us

As advice meant for
Each of us, personally.

They permit us to locate,
With perfect ease,
The true intent of the Victors.

And we are also
Protected from

Falling off the high cliff
Of the Great Mistake.

[59]
DE LTA BU'I GZHUNG 'DI NI, KHYAD CHOS SAM CHE BA BZHI
DANG LDAN TE, GDAMS PA 'DI LA BRTEN NAS RGYAL BAS CHOS
TSUL JI SNYAD {%SNYED} CIG GSUNGS PA THAMS CAD LAS, KHA
CIG NI LAM GYI GTZO BO, KHA CIG NI DE'I YAN LAG STON BYED
DU SHES NAS DNGOS DANG BRGYUD PA CI RIGS KYI SGO NAS
'TSANG RGYA BA'I CHA RKYEN DU GO BAR 'GYUR BAS NA, **BSTAN
PA THAMS CAD 'GAL MED** DU **RTOGS PA**'I CHE BA **DANG**,

The classic genre that we have been referring to here has
four different features, or we can say types of greatness.
The first of these is what we refer to as "greatness in
*allowing us to grasp that each one of the teachings is completely
compatible with all the others."*

What this means is that—if we allow ourselves to rely
upon the advices on the steps—then we can come to
understand how each & every one of the entire amount of
teachings ever granted by the Victorious Buddhas acts—
either directly or indirectly—to support our achievement
of final enlightenment. That is, we see how some of these
teachings present principal paths to those goals; while
others present ancillaries to these paths.

[60]
MDO SNGAGS KYI GSUNG RAB RNAMS DANG DE'I DGONGS
'GREL GYI BSTAN BCOS RNAMS BSHAD CHOS TZAM DU BZUNG
NAS NYAMS SU LEN RGYU DE DAG GI DON LAS GZHAN ZHIG NA
YOD PAR 'DZIN PA'I LOG RTOG RNAMS LDOG STE,

The second kind of greatness here is that the steps *make
it possible for* each & every one of *the classic teachings of the
Buddha* to *strike us as advice meant for each of us, personally.*
That is, we are able to put a stop to the mistaken idea
where we hold that the high teachings of Lord Buddha—

the various open & secret teachings—and the classical commentaries which clarify the intent of these teachings too are simply general books of instruction; and that when we are looking for something we can use in our own personal practice, we will have to seek it somewhere else than in the ideas of these teachings.

[61]
GSUNG RAB DGONGS 'GREL DANG BCAS PA'I BRJOD BYA MTHA' DAG NYAMS SU LEN GYI GO RIM DANG MTHUN PAR BSHES GNYEN BSTEN TSUL NAS ZHI LHAG GI BAR BSDUS NAS DPYAD SGOM DANG 'DZEG {%'JOG} SGOM CI RIGS KYI SGO NAS NYAMS SU LEN TSUL SHES PAR 'GYUR BAS NA, **GSUNG RAB** THAMS CAD **GDAMS PAR 'CHAR BA**'I CHE BA **DANG**,

Which is to say, we come to see how the entire content of the high speech of the Enlightened Ones, along with the commentaries which clarify its intent, are completely consistent with the order of the steps that we will need to take in our own personal practice. And we see how this practice will involve either analytical meditation or fixed meditation—whichever the case may be—upon the steps in this grand summary, which stretches from how to study with a spiritual friend, on up to the final topics of meditative quietude combined with special insight.

[62]
DE LTAR GSUNG RAB THAMS CAD GDAMS NGAG GI MCHOG YIN KYANG BLO MA SBYANGS PA'I LAS DANG PO BAS GZHUNG CHE BA DE DAG GI DGONGS DON RANG STOBS KYIS RTOGS NAS NYAMS SU LAN {%LEN} MI SHES PAS,

The third sort of greatness then is that the steps *permit us to realize, with perfect ease, the true intent of the Victors.* That is, it may well be the case that each & every example of the high speech of the Buddhas represents the highest of advices that we could ever be granted. Those of us who are beginners though—those of us who have yet to train our minds sufficiently—would not on our own immediately be able to grasp, and then put into actual practice, the true intent of these great classics.

[63]
DE DAG GI DGONGS DON RNAMS 'DUS PA'I BLA MA'I MAN NGAG BYANG CHUB LAM GYI RIM PA 'DI LTA BU LA BRTEN NAS GZHUNG CHE BA DE RNAMS KYI DGONGS DON LEGS PAR RTOGS PAR 'GYUR BAS NA, **RGYAL BA'I DGONGS PA BDE BLAG** TU RTOGS PA'I CHE BA DANG,

As such, we will need to rely upon a teaching like these steps of the path to enlightenment, shared with us as words of advice from our own Lama, since these very steps incorporate all the intended ideas of those classics. This then leads us to an excellent realization of what these great books really mean to say.

[64]
DE LTAR **RNYED PA'**I TSE SANGS RGYAS KYI BKA' THAMS CAD DNGOS **DANG** BRGYUD PA CI RIGS KYI SGO NAS 'TSANG RGYA BA'I THABS SU GO NAS 'TSANG RGYA BA'I THABS MI STON PA'I SANGS RGYAS KYI BKA' MED PAR SHES TE,

The fourth and final type of greatness here is that *we are also protected from falling off the high cliff of the Great Mistake.* What this means is that—once we have then been able to *locate* that true intent of the classics—we can grasp that each & every word ever uttered by the Enlightened Ones represents a means of reaching Buddhahood, whether that means is direct or indirect. This then helps us appreciate that, in fact, there does not exist any statement of the Buddha which was not presented as a means of attaining enlightenment.

[65]
GSUNG RAB DE DAG LA GDUL BYA'I DBANG GIS BRJOD BYA CUNG ZAD RE MI MTHUN PA DANG MCHOG DMAN YOD KYANG,

That is, with regard to the content of these high teachings

of the Enlightened One, there do in fact appear to be some statements that are slightly at odds with each other; and that certain teachings would seem to be higher, and others lower—all dictated by the capacity of the particular disciples involved.

[66]
THAMS CAD 'TSANG RGYA BA'I THABS STON PA TZAM LA KHYAD PAR MED PAR NGES NAS CHOS SPONG BA'I LAS MI 'BYUNG BA STE, **NYES SPYOD CHEN PO'I G-YANG SA LAS KYANG SRUNG** BA'I CHE BA BZHI [f. 4a] DANG LDAN PA'I PHYIR RO,,

Through studying and practicing the steps though, we come to realize that there is absolutely no difference between any of these teachings: none of them presents anything but how to become enlightened ourselves. And with this realization, we can avoid ever collecting that most terrifying karma of rejecting the Dharma. These then are the four types of greatness that the teachings on the steps possess.

Right to put into practice

[67]
GSUM PA LA GNYIS, CHE BA DE LDAN GYI CHOS 'DI NYAMS SU LEN RIGS PA DANG, NYAMS SU BLANGS PA'I PHAN YON NO,,

This brings us to our third point from above: the purpose of our explanation. Here we have two topics: showing how appropriate it is then to put into practice this teaching, with its different types of greatness; and the benefits we receive from putting things into actual practice this way.

[68]
DANG PO NI, DE PHYIR RGYA BOD MKHAS PA'I SOGS BZHI STE,

The first of these two is found in the four lines [of the

Tibetan] which include "as such…masters in both India and Tibet."

[69]

(9)
,DE PHYIR RGYA BOD MKHAS PA'I SKYE BO NI,
,SKAL LDAN DU MAS BSTEN PA'I GDAMS PA MCHOG
,SKYES BU GSUM GYI LAM GYI RIM PA YIS,
,YID RAB MI 'PHROG DPYOD LDAN SU ZHIG YOD,

As such, the steps
Are a supreme form
Of instruction

Relied upon
By a great many people
Of sufficient goodness—
By great masters—
In both India and Tibet.

Where could we find
A person with intelligence
Whose heart wasn't
Completely stolen away

By these steps of the path
Designed for persons
Of three types of capacity?

[70]
SNGAR BSHAD PA'I CHE BA DE LTAR YOD PA'I RGYU MTSAN DE'I PHYIR NA, RGYA GAR DANG BOD KYI MKHAS PA'I SKYE BO NI SKAL BA DANG LDAN PA DU MAS NYAMS LEN DU BSTEN PA'I GDAMS PA MCHOG TU GYUR PA SKYES BU CHUNG 'BRING CHE GSUM GYI LAM GYI RIM PA YIS NI YID RAB TU MI 'PHROG PA'I RNAM DPYOD DANG LDAN PA SU ZHIG YOD DE MED DO,,

As such—that is, for the reason that these *steps* do

indeed possess the types of greatness that we have just described—*where could we ever find a person with intelligence whose heart wasn't completely stolen away by* them? Surely we could not.

These *steps of the path, designed for persons of three types* of *capacity*—lesser, medium, and greater—do represent, after all, *a supreme form of instruction.* And that instruction has been *"relied upon,"* or put into practice, *by a great many people of sufficient goodness—by great masters—in both India and Tibet.*

All the benefits, in a compact form

[71]

GNYIS PA NI, GSUNG RAB KUN GYI SNYING PO SOGS BZHI STE,

Our second point here—the benefits we receive from putting things into actual practice this way—is presented in the four lines [of Tibetan] which include "the deepest heart of all the high speech of the Enlightened Ones."

[72]

(10)
,GSUNG RAB KUN GYI SNYING PO BSDU BSDU BA,
,TSUL 'DI THUN RE STON DANG NYAN PAS KYANG,
,DAM CHOS 'CHAD DANG THOS PA'I PHAN YON TSOGS,
,RLABS CHEN SDUD PAR NGES PAS DE DON BSAM,

> **This then is a system**
> **Which embodies the**
> **Deepest heart**
>
> **Of all the high speech**
> **Of the Enlightened Ones.**

When we teach or listen
To the steps
Even just a single time,

We are able thus
To obtain,
With perfect certainty,
And with powerful efficiency,

All the benefits
Of explaining,

And listening to,
All the holy Dharma.

Contemplate then
This point well.

[73]
THEG PA CHE CHUNG GI **GSUNG RAB KUN GYI SNYING PO BSDU BSDU BA**'I GZHUNG GI **TSUL 'DI** NI, LAN MANG DU LTA CI **THUN RE STON** PA **DANG** LAN RE **NYAN PAS KYANG** GZHUNG CHE BA NAS **DAM CHOS 'CHAD** PA **DANG THOS PA'I PHAN YON** GYI **TSOGS RLABS CHEN** 'BYUNG BAR GSUNGS PA DE RNAMS **SDUD PAR NGES PAS** SO,,

This then is a system of classical knowledge *which embodies the deepest heart of all the high speech of the Enlightened Ones:* all the classics of both the lesser and the greater ways. And suppose we *teach or listen to the steps* not just a large number of times, but *even just a single time.* It is stated that *we* can *thus, with powerful efficiency, obtain all the benefits of explaining, and listening to, all the holy Dharma* taught in the great classics of Buddhism. That is, *we are able—with perfect certainty*—to accumulate all these benefits.

[74]
RGYU MTSAN DES NA, **DE'I DON** YID LA **BSAM** PAR BYA'O, ,ZHES
PA NI DON BSDU BA'I SGO NAS GDAMS PA'O,,

For this reason *then* we are instructed to *"Contemplate this point well,* in our hearts." This last is a summary advice to us.

[75]
BSDU BSDU BA NI GSUNG RAB THAMS CAD KYI GNAD BSDUS PA
DANG DE YANG MDOR BSDUS TE BSTAN PA'I DON NO,,

The phrase where the steps are described as "the deepest heart" is meant first of all to convey that they incorporate the crucial points of each & every one of the high teachings of the Buddhas. It is also meant to indicate that the steps provide these points in a very compact form.

Preliminaries to the path

[76]
GNYIS PA GZHUNG GI DON BSHAD PA LA,

This then brings us to our second major division from above: explaining the meaning of the actual text of the work.

[77]
MCHOD BRJOD SOGS NI, GZHUNG GI YAN LAG YIN LA, 'DIR
GZHUNG DON DNGOS KYI DBANG DU BYAS TE 'CHAD PA LA
GNYIS, THUN MONG BA DANG, THUN MONG MA YIN PA'I LAM
LA BSLAB TSUL LO,,

Now the offering of praise and other steps that we've covered so far are only ancillaries to the actual work. Here we will move on to an explanation of the actual meaning of the text itself. This comes in two divisions: an explanation of how we practice the path of the shared steps, followed by an explanation of how we practice the path of the unique steps.

[78]
DANG PO LA GNYIS, SNGON 'GRO DANG, DNGOS GZHI'O, ,DANG PO NI, DE NAS 'DI PHYI'I LEGS TSOGS SOGS BRGYAD DE,

The first of these divisions has two points of its own: the preliminaries, and the actual instruction. The first of these is presented in the eight lines [of the Tibetan] which include "the entire collection, then, of the good things that could ever happen in this life, or in our future lives":

[79]

(11)
,DE NAS 'DI PHYI'I LEGS TSOGS JI SNYED PA'I,
,RTEN 'BREL LEGS PAR 'GRIG PA'I RTZA BA NI,
,LAM STON BSHES GNYEN DAM PA 'BAD PA YIS,
,BSAM DANG SBYOR BAS TSUL BZHIN BSTEN PA RU,

The specific root cause then
For getting off
To a good start

In the entire collection
Of the good things

That could ever happen
In this life,
Or in our future lives,

Is our holy spiritual friend,
The one who shows us
The path.

And then with great efforts
We need to rely
Upon that Lama

In our thoughts
And in our actual actions.

[80]

(12)

,MTHONG NAS SROG GI PHYIR YANG MI GTONG BAR,
,BKA' BZHIN SGRUB PA'I MCHOD PAS MNYES PAR BYED,
,RNAL 'BYOR NGAS KYANG NYAMS LEN DE LTAR BGYIS,
,THAR 'DOD KHYED KYANG DE BZHIN BSKYANG 'TSAL LO,

Seeing this,
We see that we must
Please them with the offering

Of accomplishing everything
They have commanded us to do,
Without ever giving it up,
Even at the cost of our life.

I, the deep practitioner,
Have accomplished my practice
This way;

And you who hope for freedom
Should do your practice
The same.

[81]

LAM RIM YONGS RDZOGS DANG DE'I CHA SHAS TZAM LAS SU
BLANGS PA LAS KYANG PHAN YON CHEN PO YOD TSUL BSAM PA
SOGS SNGON DU BTANG STE **DE NAS** 'DI LTAR NYAMS SU BLANG
BAR BYA'O, ,ZHES MTSAMS SBYAR RO,,

These stanzas represent a certain kind of segue, advising
us first for example to give some thought to how there
are great benefits to putting into practice the steps of the
path in their entirety—or even just any small portion of
them. And *then* we think to ourselves, "Well then, I will
certainly give these steps an actual try!"

[82]
PHAN YON DE LTAR MTHONG BA DES, **'DI DANG PHYI** MA'I
LEGS TSOGS JI SNYED MCHIS **PA'I RTEN 'BREL LEGS PAR 'GRIG
PA**R 'GYUR BA'**I RTZA BA NI**, RANG LA **LAM STON** PA'I DGE BA'I
BSHES GNYEN DAM PAR SHES PAR BYAS TE,

A person who has seen that this is how the benefits come
starts off with the following thoughts. There is a *specific
root cause for getting off to a good start in the entire collection
of* all *the good things that could ever happen in this life, or in
our future lives.* We need to come to the understanding
that this root is *our holy spiritual friend:* our goodness
friend, *the one who shows us the path.*

[83]
'BAD PA [f. 4b] DRAG PO **YIS**, BLA MA LA SKYON RTOG GI BLO
BKAG NAS DAD PA SKYE CI THUB BYED PA'I SGO NAS **BSAM** PAS
BSTEN PA **DANG**,

And then with great, fierce *efforts we need to rely upon that
Lama in our thoughts.* This is done first by putting a
stop to any perceptions we might have that this teacher
possesses any kinds of faults; and then by cultivating as
much faith as we can in them.

[84]
BLA MA MNYES PA SGO MTHA' DAG NAS BSGRUB CING MA
MNYES PA NAM YANG MI BSGRUB PA DANG, LUS KYIS BKUR
ZHING NGAG GIS BSTOD PA SOGS DANG, CI GSUNG BKA' BZHIN
DU SGRUB PA'I SGO NAS **SBYOR BAS TSUL BZHIN** DU **BSTEN PA
RU** STE

With this we begin our study with this Lama, relying
upon them properly *in our actual actions.* This involves
undertaking everything we can that pleases them, and
never doing anything which does not please them. We
honor them for example with the actions we undertake,
and speak well of them in our words. We rely upon them
by carrying out everything they have asked us to do, just
as they have asked us to do it.

[85]
BSTEN PA LA RAG YAS {%LAS} PAR **MTHONG NAS** RKYEN CUNG
ZAD TZAM DU MA ZAD, **SROG GI PHYIR YANG MI GTONG BAR
BKA' BZHIN** DU **SGRUB PA'I MCHOD PAS MNYES PAR BYED**
DGOS SO,,

We *see* that all our goals depend upon relying upon
our Teacher in this way; then *we see that we must*
absolutely *please them with the offering of accomplishing
everything they have commanded us to do.* And we
continue this behavior *without ever giving it up,* not
just for some small reason, but *even at the cost of
our life.*

[86]
DE'I MJUG TU, RJE'I GSUNG 'BUM THOR BU LAS, **RNAL 'BYOR
NGAS KYANG NYAMS LEN DE LTAR** BYAS, ,**THAR 'DOD KHYED
KYANG DE BZHIN BSKYANG 'TSAL LO**, ,ZHES 'BYUNG BA NI,
RJE'I GSUNG DNGOS YIN LA,

After this section, we see certain lines added here from
the collection of briefer works of Lord Tsongkapa. These
words are advice to us from the Lord's own lips, and
they go like this:

> *I, the deep practitioner,*
> *Have accomplished my practice*
> *This way;*

> *And you who hope for freedom*
> *Should do your practice*
> *The same.*[15]

---

[15] *Do your practice the same:* These lines are indeed found in our text as
it appears in the collection of briefer works, except that untypically Je
Rinpoche has referred to himself there with the high honorific verb *bgyis.*
See f. 56a (B10, S05275-59).

[87]
CHOS SPYOD LAS, RJE BTZUN BLA MAS NYAMS LEN DE LTAR
MDZAD, ,THAR 'DOD BDAG KYANG DE BZHIN BSKYANG 'TSAL
LO, ,ZHES 'BYUNG BA NI,

In the traditional monastery prayer manuals, we see
these lines as—

The holy Lamas
Have accomplished their practice
This way;

And I,
Who hope for freedom,

Will do my practice
The same.

[88]
PHYIS GZHAN GYIS BSGYUR BA STE, DON GO SLA ZHING PHYI
MA GZHAN LA'ANG SBYOR,

This is a later adaptation of the original lines by other
parties, and is easily understood. It can be applied in later
lines of our original verses here, as may be appropriate to
the circumstances.[16]

[89]
BLA MA'I MTSAN NYID, BSTEN TSUL SOGS LAM RIM SOGS NAS

---

[16] *As may be appropriate:* For a typical prayer-book use of the alternate
lines, see for example f. 181b of *A Compendium of Liturgical Texts Utilized
at the Various Major Monasteries* (B15, S00207). The point is that—when
monastics or us modern people sit, especially together, and read Je
Rinpoche's text out loud—these particular lines are not (as for Je
Tsongkapa) a statement of what we have accomplished, but of what we
hope to accomplish. Still, on an advanced level, seeing ourselves as him
and reciting his words as he would himself itself represents a traditional,
powerful practice of the steps of the path.

SHES PAR BYA'O,,

The traditional definition of a Lama; how to study with them properly; and other details are something you should learn from sources such as the more detailed texts on the steps of the path.[17]

Using our leisure & fortune

[90]
GNYIS PA LA GNYIS, DAL 'BYOR LA SNYING PO LEN PAR BSKUL BA DANG, SNYING PO JI LTAR LEN TSUL LO,,

This brings us to our second point here—the actual instruction. Here we have two parts: strong advice that we try to get the very essence out of the leisure & fortune that we have; and then a description of just how we derive this essence.

[91]
DANG PO NI, DAL BA'I RTEN 'DI YID BZHIN NOR SOGS TE,

The first of these is expressed in the lines that include, "This body & mind of leisure is more valuable than a wishing jewel":

[92]
(13a)
,DAL BA'I RTEN 'DI YID BZHIN NOR LAS LHAG

---

[17] *More detailed texts:* The most detailed and accessible source of the kind mentioned here is certainly *A Gift of Liberation, Thrust into the Palm of Your Hand,* by the great Pabongka Rinpoche, Dechen Nyingpo (1878-1941) (B12, S00004). The section mentioned begins at f. 66a of the Tibetan; an excellent English translation is available (E1), and the same section can be accessed by looking for the same Tibetan folio number inserted in the translation.

,'DI 'DRA RNYED PA DA RES TZAM ZHIG YIN,

This body & mind of leisure
Is more valuable than
A wishing jewel.

Our present life
Is the only one in which
We've been able
To find them.

[93]
DAL BRGYAD 'BYOR BCU LDAN PA'I SGO NAS CHOS SGRUB PA LA
KHOS {%KHOM} PAS NA **DAL BA'I RTEN** KHYAD PAR CAN **'DI** NI,

Now we possess *a body & mind of* exceptional *"leisure"*
in that we possess the time & opportunity to practice
the Dharma, given that we have available to us the eight
classical forms of leisure,[18] and the ten classical forms of
fortune.[19]

---

[18] *Eight forms of leisure:* These may be found in many sources; here is the
presentation as given by the great Fifth Dalai Lama, Ngawang Lobsang
Gyatso (1617-1682), in his famed work on the steps of the path, *The Word
of Gentle Voice* (see f. 16b, B4, S05637):

The eight forms of leisure consist of being free of absences of opportunity:

    (1) holding mistaken viewpoints about life;
    (2-4) being born into the three lower realms—the hell realms,
            as a craving spirit, or as an animal;
    (5) being born into a world that no Buddha has come to;
    (6) being born into an "outlying land," one that has
              not yet been reached by the teachings of Buddhism;
    (7) being born deaf & dumb; and
    (8) being born as a long-lived worldly god.

[19] *Ten forms of fortune:* These are listed in the same source by the Great
Fifth (again see f. 16b) as follows:
The ten forms of fortune include two sections, the first relating to
        ourselves personally:
    (1) Being born as a human;

[94]
YID BZHIN GYI **NOR** BU RIN PO CHE **LAS** KYANG **LHAG** PA 'DI
'DRA BA NI SNGAR YANG YANG RNYED PA MA YIN GYI **RNYED
PA** DUS **DA RES TZAM ZHIG YIN** NO,,

Leisures and fortunes *such as these,* which are *more valuable*
even *than* one of those gems which is *a wishing jewel,* are
not something that we have ever—in the past—been able
to obtain, on a frequent basis. Rather, *our present life is the
only* time *we've been able to find them.*

[95]
DES RNYED NA DON CHE BAR MA ZAD, RNYED PAR DKA' BAR
BSTAN TO,,

All this is meant to indicate that not only are these
leisures & fortunes something of great value; but they are
also extremely difficult to find.

[96]
YID BZHIN GYI NOR BU LAS LHAG TSUL NI NOR BU LAS DGOS
'DOD 'BYUNG YANG TSE 'DI'I GNAS SKABS KYI 'DOD DON YIN LA,

(2) Being born into a "central land"—a place that has been
    reached by the teachings of Buddhism;

(3) Being born with all of ones sense organs complete;

(4) Not having committed extremely serious bad karma;

(5) Being born in a place where the people have faith
    in the Dharma, and are willing to support practitioners.

The second section relates to our more general environment:

(6) A Buddha has come to our world, and not yet displayed
    their final nirvana, or passing away [we do not
    technically possess this one, but do have qualified

teachers present in our life];

(7) Buddhas, or their representatives, are teaching in our world;

(8) The teachings of the Buddhas have not degenerated;

(9) People are following the teachings, having observed their
    beneficial results; and

(10) There are other beings who have compassion for us here.

Just how is it that these things are more valuable even than a wishing jewel? When we say that these kinds of jewels supply us with what we need, what we're actually talking about is the temporary needs of this current lifetime.

[97]
RTEN 'DI LA BRTEN NAS MNGON MTHO TZAM DU MA ZAD, NGES LEGS THAR PA DANG THAMS CAD MKHYEN PA BSGRUBS NA'ANG THOB NUS PAR GSUNGS PA'I PHYIR NA LHAG GO

These leisures & fortunes though are even more precious, because—as it has been stated in the teachings—by relying on this current body & mind that we possess, we can not only reach a higher rebirth, but are even able to attain "definite good": which is to say, freedom & omniscience.[20]

[98]
,DE LTAR RNYED DKA' ZHING RNYED NA DON CHE BA'I DAL 'BYOR GYI RTEN 'DI DON MED DU MI BTANG BAR 'DI LA RANG GIS CI NUS KYI SGO NAS CHOS BYA BA'I DAM BCA' BRTAN PO BYA'O,,

The point is that we all need to make a firm resolution to carry out the Dharma to the very best of our ability, and not waste—in meaningless pursuits—this body & mind with its leisures & fortunes, so difficult to acquire and, once acquired, so very valuable.

---

[20] *Freedom and omniscience:* When freedom is presented this way, as the counterpart of omniscience or total Buddhahood, it refers to a kind of nirvana in which we have reached only our personal goals.

How we group the teachings

[99]
GNYIS PA SNYING PO JI LTAR LEN TSUL LA [f. 5a] GNYIS, LAM GYI DBANG DU BYAS PA'I GSUNG RAB RNAMS 'DU TSUL DANG, NYAMS SU LEN TSUL DNGOS SO, ,DANG PO NI,

Which brings us to our second point from above—a description of just how we derive the essence out of the leisure & fortune that we have. Here we have two topics: how we group the high teachings with regard to the path; and then the actual way in which we go about deriving the essence mentioned. We begin with the first.

[100]
SANGS RGYAS BCOM LDAN 'DAS KYIS CHOS KYI PHUNG PO JI SNYED CIG GSUNGS PA NI SEMS CAN GYI DON DU YIN LA,

Now all the huge mountains of Dharma that the Buddha, the Conqueror, has ever spoken were all meant to help living beings.

[101]
DE YANG MNGON MTHO NGES LEGS GNYIS LAS, MNGON MTHO LAS BRTZAMS TE GTZO BOR GSUNGS PA RNAMS SKYES BU CHUNG NGU DNGOS SAM DE DANG THUN MONG BA'I CHOS SKOR DU 'DU ZHING,

Dividing our spiritual goals into the two of achieving the higher rebirths, and definite good, those teachings that were primarily presented in the context of achieving a higher rebirth are included into the collection of instructions for people of lesser capacity. These could be included, by the way, directly; or as part of a greater body of teachings that incorporate these advices.

[102]
NGES LEGS LA GNYIS LAS THAR PA LA BRTZAMS TE GTZO BOR

GSUNGS PA RNAMS SKYES BU 'BRING DNGOS SAM DE DANG THUN MONG BA'I CHOS SKOR DU 'DU LA,

What we call "definite good" involves two different parts. Those teachings that were given primarily in the context of reaching freedom are included directly into the collection of instructions for people of medium capacity; or again as part of a greater body of teachings that incorporate these advices.

[103]
THAMS CAD MKHYEN PA SGRUB PA LAS BRTZAMS TE GSUNGS PA THAMS CAD SKYES BU CHEN PO'I CHOS SKOR DU 'DU BA YIN NO,,

Those teachings that were given primarily in the context of achieving omniscience are all grouped into the collection of instructions for people of great capacity.

[104]
'DIR SKYES BU CHUNG 'BRING DANG THUN MONG BA'I LAM 'GA' ZHIG SKYES BU CHEN PO'I LAM GYI YAN LAG TU DGOS PA DER 'KHRID PA YIN GYI, SKYES BU CHUNG 'BRING DNGOS KYI LAM LA 'KHRID PA NI MA YIN TE,

Here we are going to lead you along a number of paths which are shared with people of lesser and medium capacities, as they are needed as ancillaries to the path of those of greater capacity. But it is not that we will be taking you along the actual paths for people of lesser or medium capacity.

[105]
MNGON MTHO TZAM ZHIG DON GNYER GYI BLO DE SKYES BU CHUNG NGU'I LAM DNGOS DANG, RANG DON DU THAR PA TZAM ZHIG DON GNYER GYI BLO DE SKYES BU 'BRING GI LAM DNGOS YIN PAS, DER 'KHRID NA NI SKYES BU CHEN PO'I LAM GYI GO SAR {%GOL SAR} 'KHRID PA'I SKYON DU 'GYUR BA'I PHYIR RO,,

The state of mind in which we aspire to no more than gaining higher rebirths is the actual path for persons of lesser capacity; whereas the state of mind where we aspire for no more than freedom for our own benefit is the actual path for people of medium capacity. As such, if we were to lead a person down one of these lower paths, we would be making the mistake of actually leading you astray.

[106]
'O NA, DE GNYIS DANG THUN MONG BA'I LAM JI LTA BU ZHE NA,

"Well then," one may respond, "just what does it mean when you say that a path is shared with a person of one of these two capacities?"

[107]
SDIG SPONG DGE BA SGRUB PA'I SGO NAS MNGON MTHO DON GNYER GYI BLO DE, SKYES BU CHUNG NGU DANG THUN MONG BA'I LAM DANG, 'KHOR BA LAS GROL 'DOD KYI SGO NAS THAR PA DON GNYER GYI BLO DE SKYES BU 'BRING DANG THUN MONG BA'I LAM YIN TE, DE GNYIS KA'ANG BYANG SEMS KYI RGYUD LA YOD CING, DES NYAMS SU LEN DGOS PA'I PHYIR RO,,

That state of mind where we aspire to higher rebirths by means of giving up bad deeds, and accomplishing good deeds, constitutes the path which is shared with people of lesser capacity. And that state of mind where we aspire to freedom because we want to be liberated from the cycle of pain constitutes the path which is shared with people of medium capacity. Both of these states of mind are present in the mind stream of a bodhisattva; and both of them must be practiced by a bodhisattva.

[108]
GAL TE SKYES BU CHUNG 'BRING GI LAM GNYIS SKYES BU CHEN PO'I LAM GYI GOL SA YIN NA, DE'I GEGS SAM MI MTHUN PHYOGS YIN PA'I PHYIR 'TSANG RGYA BA'I THABS KYANG MA YIN PAR

'GYUR RO ZHE NA,

And then one might continue with the following question: "If the practice of the paths for people of lesser and medium capacity represent going astray—for people on the path for those of greater capacity—then since this practice represents a blockage, or an impediment, then it cannot be the case that it constitutes a method for reaching enlightenment."

[109]
SKYON MED DE, LAM DE GNYIS SKYES BU CHEN PO MYUR DU 'TSANG RGYA BA'I LAM GYI GOL SA YIN PAS DE 'TSANG RGYA BA'I THABS MA YIN KYANG, NYAN RANG RNAMS RIM GYIS RGYUD SMIN TE 'TSANG RGYA [f. 5b] BA'I THABS SU 'GYUR BA LA 'GAL BA CI YANG MED PA'I PHYIR RO,,

And yet there is no such problem. Those two particular paths do represent going astray, from the path that people of greater capacity need to use to reach enlightenment with speed. As such, in this context we can say that they are not methods for becoming enlightened. But there is no contradiction at all in saying that these are methods for becoming enlightened from the point of view that they serve to ripen—in stages—the minds of the listeners and self-made buddhas.

[110]
DE YANG RANG NYID GCIG PU ZHI BDE DON GNYER GYI BLO LTA BU LA GTZO BOR DGONGS PA'O,,

The discussion we have engaged in just now is mainly posited on something like the state of mind where we are hoping to reach the happiness of peace only for ourselves, alone.

A meditation on death

[111]
GNYIS PA LA GSUM, SKYES BU CHUNG NGU DANG THUN MONG
BA'I LAM, 'BRING DANG THUN MONG BA'I LAM, CHEN PO'I LAM
DNGOS SO,,

With this we have reached our second topic, the actual way in which we go about deriving the essence out of the leisure & fortune that we possess. Here we have three sections: the path which is shared with those of lesser capacity; the path which is shared with those of medium capacity; and then the actual path for people of greater capacity.

[112]
DANG PO LA GNYIS, PHYI MA DON GNYER GYI BLO BSKYED PA,
PHYI MA'I BDE THABS BSTEN PA'O,,

The first of these three has two parts of its own: giving birth to the state of mind where we are aspiring to goals that will come after we die; and how to engage in methods that will bring us happiness after this death.

[113]
DANG PO LA GNYIS, 'CHI BA MI RTAG PA BSAM PA DANG, NGAN
'GRO'I SDUG BSNGAL BSAM PA'O, ,DANG PO NI, RNYED DKA' 'JIG
SLA SOGS BZHI STE,

Finally here, the first of the two parts includes two sections of its own: the contemplation on our impermanence, in the form of our death; and then the contemplation upon the sufferings of the lower realms. The first of these is found in the four lines [of the Tibetan] which include "It is hard to find, and easily destroyed":

[114]

(13b-14)
,RNYED DKA' 'JIG SLA NAM MKHA'I GLOG DANG 'DRA,
,TSUL 'DI BSAMS NAS 'JIG RTEN BYA BA KUN,

,SBUN PA 'PHYAR BA BZHIN DU RTOGS GYUR NAS,
,NYIN MTSAN KUN TU SNYING PO LEN PA DGOS,
,RNAL 'BYOR NGAS KYANG NYAMS LEN DE LTAR BGYIS,
,THAR 'DOD KHYED KYANG DE BZHIN BSKYANG 'TSAL LO,

> It is hard to find,
> And easily destroyed—
> Like lightning in the sky.

> Devoting some thought
> To this, we need to realize

> That all our worldly activities
> Are like the chaff we remove
> From grains of wheat,

> And spend every hour
> Of the day & night
> Working to get
> The very essence
> Out of it.

> I, the deep practitioner,
> Have accomplished my practice
> This way;

> And you who hope for freedom
> Should do your practice
> The same.

[115]
RGYU, NGO BO, DPE'I SGO NAS **RNYED** PAR **DKA'** ZHING, 'CHI
RKYEN MANG BAS **'JIG** PAR **SLA** BA NI,

A body & mind such as the one we now possess is *hard*

72

to find, from three different viewpoints: its cause; its essential nature; and from the point of view of applicable metaphors.[21] And because there are many things in the world that can kill us, this same body & mind is *easily destroyed.*

[116]
DPER NA, **NAM MKHA'I GLOG** MYUR DU 'JIG PA **DANG 'DRA** BA'I **TSUL 'DI BSAMS NAS** DGRA 'DUL GNYEN SKYONG SOGS **'JIG RTEN** GYI **BYA BA KUN**

We can, for example, *devote some thought to* how similar our body & mind is to *lightning in the sky,* which disappears so instantly. And this will lead us to a certain perception about *all the worldly activities* we are engaged in: things like making sure our enemies' lives get worse, while our friends & relatives are sustained & supported.

[117]
DPER NA, SNYING PO MED PA'I SHUN PA'I SPUN {%**SBUN**} **PA** '**PHYAR BA BZHIN DU** DON MED PAR **RTOGS** PAR **GYUR NAS** NYIN MTSAN KUN TU RTEN 'DI LA **SNYING PO LEN PA DGOS** SO,,

All of these efforts are—to use an example—*like the chaff we remove from grains of wheat:* it is just the outside skin, with nothing substantial inside of it. Just so, all those

---

[21] *Three different viewpoints:* These are covered in many of the more detailed presentations of the steps of the path. The *Path of Bliss,* for example, composed by His Holiness the First Panchen Lama, Lobsang Chukyi Gyeltsen (1565-1662), briefly describes the "cause" here as beginning with a prior practice of completely pure morality, accompanied by practices such as the perfection of giving, and then also immaculate prayers or intentions. As for essential nature, a fully functional human being is simply statistically extremely rare, among all the possible forms of life. Finally, the occurrence of a healthy, human body & mind can be compared to the metaphor of a star shining in broad daylight: impossible almost by definition. See the discussion beginning from f. 7b (B13, S05944).

worldly activities are completely meaningless. *We need to realize* this, *and* then *spend every hour of* our life—*day & night*—*working to get the very essence out of* this body & mind we possess.

Sufferings in the lower realms after we die

[118]
GNYIS PA NGAN 'GRO'I SDUG BSNGAL BSAM PA NI, SHI NAS NGAN 'GROR MI SKYE ZHES PA STE,

Which brings us to that second point: the contemplation upon the sufferings of the lower realms. This is described in the line that includes "I won't have to take birth into the lower realms":

[119]

(15a)
,SHI NAS NGAN 'GROR MI SKYE'I GDENG MED CING,

> **I have no guarantee that,**
> **Once I do die,**
> **I won't have to take birth**
> **Into the lower realms.**

[120]
DE LTAR 'CHI BA MI RTAG PAR MA ZAD, **SHI NAS** LAS DKAR NAG GNYIS KYIS JI LTAR 'PHANGS PA BZHIN SKYE BA LEN DGOS LA,

Not only are we plagued by impermanence, in the form of our mortality; *once we* do *die,* we must take a rebirth, as dictated by the two of the white or black karma that we may have collected.

[121]
DE NI DGE BA'I LAS KYIS BDE 'GROR SKYE ZHING BDE BA MYONG LA, MI DGE BA'I LAS KYIS NGAN 'GROR SKYE ZHING SDUG BSNGAL MYONG NGO,,

How this works is that—if we have collected good karma in this current life—then afterwards we are born into one of the higher realms, and experience happiness; while if we have collected bad karma, we are born into to one of the lower realms, and experience suffering.

[122]
BDAG GIS NI BDE SKYO {%SKYE} 'GROR SKYE BA'I RGYU CHER MA BSGRUBS LA, NGAN 'GROR SKYE BA'I NI MANG DU BSAGS SO,,

Now it's not that I have managed in this life to accomplish a great many deeds that would cause me to be born into the realms of greater happiness; in fact, I have accumulated a great many causes to be born into the realms of misery.

[123]
DE'I PHYIR NA PHYI MAR DMYAL BA LA SOGS PA **NGAN 'GROR MI SKYE** BA**'I GDENGS** THOB PA BDAG LA **MED CING**,

And so it's not as if I have been able to secure some kind of guarantee *that* in my upcoming lifetimes *I won't have to take birth into the lower births:* into the realms of hell, or the like. In fact, I *have no* such *guarantee.*

[124]
MED PAR MA ZAD, DER SKYE BSHUGS CHE'O SNYAM NAS NGAN 'GRO'I SDUG BSNGAL YANG YANG BSAMS TE DE LAS THAR 'DOD SHUGS CAN BSKYED DO,,

And not only do I have no guarantee of not passing to these realms; rather, what I really have is more of a great likelihood that I *will* be born there. We need to be thinking in these terms; and we need to consider, over & over, the sufferings of those lower realms. And then we will be able to create, within our hearts, a powerful wish for freedom.

How to go for shelter

[125]
GNYIS PA PHYI MA'I BDE THABS LA GSUM, SKYABS 'GRO BSLAB BYA DANG BCAS PA DANG, DE LA LAS GNYIS KYI BLANG DOR LA 'JUG DGOS PA DANG, RNAM MKHYEN SGRUB PA'I RTEN BSHAD PA'O,,

Which brings us to our second part from before: how to engage in methods that will bring us happiness after the death ahead of us. This comes in the following three sections: an explanation of how to go for shelter, along with the traditional advices for this practice; an explanation of how, in this regard, we will need to learn to take up and give up, respectively, the two kinds of karma; and then a presentation on the foundation that we need to lay, in order to achieve the state of omniscience.

[126]
DANG PO NI, DE YI 'JIGS SKYOB DKON MCHOG GSUM SOGS GSUM STE,

The first of these is described in the three lines [in the Tibetan] which include "which can protect us from this terror is the Three Jewels":

[127]
(15b)
,DE YI 'JIGS SKYOB DKON MCHOG GSUM DU NGES,
,DE PHYIR SKYABS 'GRO SHIN TU BRTAN PA DANG,
,DE YI BSLAB BYA NYAMS PA MED PAR BYA,

The only shelter
Which can protect us
From this terror is—
With absolute certainty—
The Three Jewels.

To that end,
We must make sure
That our act of
Taking shelter
Is steadfast.

And then we need
To assure that we
Never digress
In the advices.

[128]
DE LTAR LAS KYI DBANG GIS NGAN 'GROR LTUNG BAR 'GYUR
BAS NGAN 'GRO **DE YI 'JIGS** PA LAS **SKYOB** PA'I SKYABS NI **DKON
MCHOG GSUM DU NGES** [f. 6a] SO,,

Thus it is that it is karma which can drag us down to the
lower realms. As such, *the only shelter which can protect
us from these terrors* of the lower realms *is, with absolute
certainty, the Three Jewels.*

[129]
DE YANG JI SKAD DU,
,SANGS RGYAS CHOS DANG DGE 'DUN TE,
,THAR PA 'DOD PA RNAMS KYI SKYABS,

We see this sentiment expressed in scripture, with the
following words—

The Buddha,
The Dharma,
And the Community:

These are the protection
For those who hope for freedom.[22]

[130]
,ZHES 'BYUNG BA LTAR, DKON MCHOG GSUM SO SO'I KHYAD PAR
DANG YON TAN SHES PA'I SGO NAS SKYABS SU 'GRO DGOS SO,,

As these lines are indicating, we need to go to the
Three Jewels for shelter by having an understanding
of both the differences and the fine qualities of
each Jewel.

[131]
'GRO TSUL YANG SNYING THAG PA NAS DKON MCHOG GSUM LA
'KHOR BA DANG NGAN SONG GI SDUG BSNGAL LAS SKYOB PA'I
NUS PA YOD PAR YID CHES PA'I SGO NAS RE LTOS 'CHA' BA'I BLO
BSKYED PA'O,,

And just how is it that we go to these three for shelter? We
need to try to develop an attitude where we put all our
hopes in the Three Jewels, believing in the very depths
of our hearts that they do possess the power to protect
us from the sufferings of the cycle of pain in general, and
more specifically those of the lower realms.

[132]
DE LTAR 'JIGS PA DE LAS SKYOB NUS PAR SHES NAS SKYOB PA **DE'I
PHYIR** DU DE GSUM LA SKYABS SU SONG BA'I **SKYABS 'GRO SHIN
TU** BSTEN {%**BRTAN**} **PA DANG** SKYABS 'GRO **DE YI BSLAB BYA**
THUN MONG BA DANG THUN MONG MA YIN PA LAM RIM SOGS
NAS BSHAD PA LA **NYAMS PA MED PAR BYA**'O,,

Once we understand, in this way, that the Three do
possess the power to protect us from these terrors, then

---

[22] These are the protection: See f. 251a of Master Chandrakirti's Seventy
Lines on Going for Shelter to the Three (S1, aTD03971).

78

to that end we must make sure that our act of taking shelter in them *is steadfast.*[23] *And then we need to assure that we never digress in* our understanding of *the advices* on how to go for shelter, as these are explained in works such as those on the steps of the path—where they describe both the common and uncommon versions of these advices.

Taking up & giving up karma

[133]
GNYIS PA NI, DE YANG DKAR NAG LAS 'BRAS SOGS TE,

Which brings us to our second section here—an explanation of how, in this regard, we will need to learn to take up and give up, respectively, the two kinds of karma. This point is expressed in the root text with the words, "And now we have to consider white & black karma":

[134]
(16)
,DE YANG DKAR NAG LAS 'BRAS LEGS BSAMS NAS,
,BLANG DOR TSUL BZHIN SGRUB LA RAG LAS SO,
,RNAL 'BYOR NGAS KYANG NYAMS LEN DE LTAR BGYIS,
,THAR 'DOD KHYED KYANG DE BZHIN BSKYANG 'TSAL LO,

And now we have to
Consider, carefully,
White & black karma,
And its consequences.

---

[23] *Our taking shelter is steadfast:* The English translation here is based on Je Rinpoche's original lines, with the relevant spelling of *brtan-pa.* Choney Lama has used the spelling *bsten-pa,* which has exactly the same pronunciation and fittingly conveys "relying completely."

We have to rely
On a practice that
Relates in a correct way

To what we take up
And what we give up.

I, the deep practitioner,
Have accomplished my practice
This way;

And you who hope for freedom
Should do your practice
The same.

[135]
DE YANG DAD PA LA SPYIR DANG BA'I DAD PA, YID CHES PA'I DAD PA, 'DOD PA'I DAD PA DANG GSUM YOD KYANG 'DIR NI GTZO BO YID CHES PA'I DAD PA STE,

And now there are, in general, three different types of faith: faith in the form of admiration; faith in the form of belief; and faith in the form of aspiration. Here what we are mainly dealing with is that in the form of belief.

[136]
DKON MCHOG GIS SKYOB PA DE YANG LAS 'BRAS LA BLANG DOR PHYIN CI LOG TU BSGRUBS NA MI 'BYUNG BAS,

Succeeding in having the Three Jewels protect us is not something that can happen if we carry out our practice in a way where we have mixed up the question of what we should take up and what we should give up, as far as karma and its consequences.

[137]
DKAR PO DGE BA DANG **NAG** PO MI DGE BA'I **LAS 'BRAS** BU DANG BCAS PA JI LTAR YIN **LEGS** PAR **BSAMS NAS** DGE BA 'BRAS

BU DANG BCAS PA LA **BLANG** BYA DANG, MI DGE 'BRAS BU DANG BCAS LA **DOR** BYAR BYED PA'I SGO NAS **TSUL BZHIN** DU **SGRUB** PA **LA RAG LAS SO**,,

As such, *we have to consider very carefully* how it is that *karma,* along with *its consequences,* work both for *"white* deeds" (referring to good deeds) *and "black* deeds" (referring to bad deeds). *What we take up* with our practice then is good deeds, along with their results; *and what we give up* is bad deeds, along with their results. Accomplishing successful sheltering then is something that *relies upon a practice that relates* to this pair *in the correct way.*

[138]
MDOR NA SANGS RGYAS KYIS DGE MI DGE SOG SOGS LAS DANG 'BRAS BU JI LTAR GSUNGS PA LA YID CHES PA'I SGO NAS BLANG DOR BYED DGOS PA'I DON NO,,

To put it briefly, the point being made here is that we all need to learn to take up, and give up, what we need to—through the act of believing in what the Buddha has said about karma and its consequences, as these relate to good deeds, bad deeds, and all the rest.

[139]
LHAG MA RJE BTZUN BLA MAS SOGS SLA'O,,

The remainder of the verse here—"the holy Lamas" and so forth—is easily understood.[24]

---

[24] *The holy Lamas:* Referring to the alternate form of the last two lines here; see the commentary to verse 12 above.

The foundation for omniscience

[140]
GSUM PA LA GNYIS, DNGOS DANG, STOBS BZHI BSTEN TSUL LO,,

Which brings us to our third section from above: a presentation on the foundation that we need to lay, in order to achieve the state of omniscience. This topic itself comes in two parts: the actual presentation, and then a description of how we use the four powers.

[141]
DANG PO NI, LAM MCHOG SGRUB LA SOGS TE,

The first of these is expressed in the lines which include "to achieve that supreme path":

[142]
(17a)
,LAM MCHOG SGRUB LA MTSAN NYID TSANG BA'I RTEN,
,MA RNYED BAR DU SA PHYOD {%CHOD} MI 'ONG [f. 56b] BAS,
,DE YI MA TSANG MED PA'I RGYU LA BSLAB,

> If we hope to achieve
> That supreme path,
> Then we need to find
>
> A body & mind
> Which possesses the
> Requisite qualities,
> All complete.
>
> Until we do,
> We won't be able to take
> Great bounds forward.
>
> And so we need
> To train ourselves
> In the necessary causes,

In no way incomplete.

[143]
KHYAD PAR DU **LAM MCHOG** RNAM MKHYEN **SGRUB** PA **LA**
TSE RING BA KHA DOG BZANG BA SOGS RNAM SMIN GYI RGYU
BRGYAD SOGS **MTSAN NYID TSANG BA'I RTEN** CI RIGS PA **MA**
RNYID {%**RNYED**} KYI **BAR DU**

More particularly, *if we hope to achieve that supreme path*
of omniscience, *then we need to find* a form of *body & mind*
which possesses the requisite qualities, all
complete. This would include for example the eight
causes that will ripen into things like a long life, and a
beautiful complexion.[25]

[144]
LAM SGRUB KYANG **SA CHOD MI 'ONG BAS**, DE 'ONG BA'I CHED
DU RTEN MTSAN NYID TSANG BA **DE YI MA TSANG MED PA'I**
RGYU SGRUB PA **LA BSLAB** PAR BYA'O,,

Until we do find these, *we won't be able to take great bounds*
forward in our practice of the path. *And so* in order to get
to this point, *we need to train ourselves in* carrying out all
the necessary causes that will allow us to achieve a body &
mind which is complete in every respect here—and *in no*
way incomplete.

[145]
RGYU NI GZHAN GYI SROG SKYOB PA, RTEN LA MAR ME 'BUL BA
SOGS [f. 6b] MANG NGO,,

There are many such causes; they include for example

---

[25] *The eight causes:* The desired results that will help us with our practice
are listed as follows by the great Jamyang Shepay Dorje, Ngawang
Tsundru (1648-1721), in his *Lineage Words of the Lama* (f. 24a, B6, S19061):
(1) a long life; (2) a beautiful complexion; (3) high social standing; (4)
complete authority; (5) perfect credibility; (6) widely recognized strength;
(7) respected personal qualities; and (8) a very healthy form.

protecting life, offering lamps on our altar, and so on.

[146]
DE'I TSE LAS 'BRAS LA BLANG DOR CI THUB BYAS KYANG, BAG
MED PA DANG NYON MONGS MANG BA'I DBANG GIS NYES PA
'BYUNG BAS SO,,

An important point here is that—regardless of how well
we carry out our attempts to do what we should do and
avoid doing what we shouldn't do, with regard to the laws
of karma and its consequences—it may happen that we
run into problems with being less mindful than we need to
be, and going through times when our mind is filled with
negative emotions.

How to use the four powers

[147]
GNYIS PA NI, SGO GSUM SDIG LTUNG SOGS TE,

Which brings us to the second part from above: a
description of how we use the four powers. This is found
in the lines that include "negative actions and downfalls
committed through the three doors":

[148]

(17b)

,SGO GSUM SDIG LTUNG DRI MAS SPAGS [*SBAGS] PA 'DI,

The fact is that
We have been dirtied
By the stain

Of negative actions
And downfalls

Committed through

The three doors of
Our actions, words, and thoughts.

[149]

(18)
,LHAG PAR LAS SGRIB SBYONG BA GNAD CHE BAS,
,RGYUN DU STOBS BZHI TSANG BAR BSTEN PA GCES,
,RNAL 'BYOR NGAS KYANG NYAMS LEN DE LTAR BGYIS,
,THAR 'DOD KHYED KYANG DE BZHIN BSKYANG 'TSAL LO,

The most crucial
Priority we have
Is to clean ourselves

Of the obstacles
We've created by
Our own karma.

As such,
We should learn to cherish
This method of
Depending constantly

Upon the practice
Where we employ
All four powers complete.

I, the deep practitioner,
Have accomplished my practice
This way;

And you who hope for freedom
Should do your practice
The same.

[150]
RANG CAG NI, LUS NGAG YID KYI **SGO GSUM** LAS NYON SPYI
DANG KHYAD PAR RANG BZHIN GYI KHA NA MA THO BA'I **SDIG**
PA DANG, BCAS PA'I KHA NA MA THO BA'I **LTUNG** BA'I **DRI MAS**
SPAGS {%**SBAGS**} **PA 'DI** NI,

Now *the fact is that* people like you and me are *dirtied by the stain,* first of all, of our general negative emotions and the karma that we have committed *through the three doors of our actions, words, and thoughts.* More specifically, we have committed *actions* that are *negative* just by their very nature; and in addition to these, *downfalls* consisting of actions that are negative because they were prohibited by our masters.

[151]
LAS DANG NYON MONGS PA'I SGRIB PA GNYIS LAS **LHAG PAR LAS** KYI **SGRIB** PA **SBYONG BA GNAD CHE BAS** NA,

As such, if we look at these two obstacles to our spiritual progress—our own bad karma and our tendency towards negative thinking—*the most crucial priority we have is to clean ourselves of* the *obstacles we've created by our own karma.*

[152]
DUS **RGYUN TU** RTEN GYI STOBS DANG, SUN 'BYIN PA'I STOBS, SLAR LDOG PA'I STOBS, GNYEN PO KUN TU SPYOD PA'I STOBS TE **STOBS BZHI**'I BSHAGS SDOM **TSANG BAR BSTEN PA**R GCES SO,,

As such, we should learn to cherish this method of depending constantly[26] upon the practice where we employ, complete, all *four powers* of confession and subsequent restraint: the power of the basis; the power of destruction; the power of restraint; and the power of the comprehensive application of the antidote.[27]

---

[26] *Depending constantly:* The peculiar preposition here in the Tibetan, *rgyun tu,* is a not uncommon variant for *rgyun du* which probably harkens back to an older secondary suffix letter *da.*

[27] *The four powers of purification:* We find a detailed explanation of these four, of course, in Pabongka Rinpoche's *Gift of Liberation* (see the section starting at f. 111b, B12, S00004). (1) The "power of the basis" involves the practice of going for refuge, in actions such as re-committing ourselves to our daily meditation practice, or daily reading of scripture. (2) The

[153]
DRI MAS SPAGS (%SBAGS) PA 'DI ZHES GZHUNG MANG POR
'BYUNG BA LTAR BYAS LA, CHOS SPYOD DU NI 'DIS ZHES 'BYUNG
NGO,,

In many editions of the root text, we see the one phrase
here as "dirtied by the stain," but we also see
"because we are dirtied by the stain" in certain of the
monastic prayer books.

[154]
STOBS BZHI'I NGOS 'DZIN DANG BSHAGS TSUL RGYAS PAR
GZHAN DU SHES PAR BYA'O,,

You should consult other sources to learn more
about exactly what each of the four powers involves,
and for details of the process of purification
through confession.

[155]
RJE BTZUN BLA MAS SOGS SNGAR BZHIN NO,,

Again, you should understand the lines about "the holy
Lamas" and so forth as we have covered them earlier on.

Contemplating suffering & its source

"power of destruction" refers to feeling strong regret for our mistaken
actions, and of course involves a strong understanding of all the bad
things those karmas will inevitably bring us. (3) The "power of restraint"
is described as the most powerful of the powers, and refers to making
a commitment to avoid repeating our mistake. In a case where the
mistaken behavior is especially chronic or easy to commit, we might
want to set a doable time limit for not repeating the action: for example,
not engaging in useless talk for the next 24 hours. (4) The "power of the
antidote" refers to particularly effective opposite actions, such as (with
useless talk) seeking out conversations with our fellow Dharma students
about the topic of emptiness.

[156]
GNYIS PA SKYES BU 'BRING DANG THUN MONG BA'I LAM NYAMS
SU LEN TSUL GNYIS, SDUG KUN GNYIS KYI NYES DMIGS PA BSAM
DGOS PA'I RGYU MTSAN DANG, BSAM TSUL DNGOS SO,,

This brings us to our second section from before: a description of the path which is shared with those of medium capacity. Here we have two topics: an explanation of the reasons why we should contemplate the problems of the two truths of suffering and its source; and then the actual method for engaging in this contemplation.

[157]
DANG PO NI, SDUG BDEN GNYES DMIGS SOGS TE,

The first of these is covered in the lines that include "the problems of the truth of suffering":

[158]
(19)
,SDUG BDEN NYES DMIGS BSAM LA MA 'BAD NA,
,THAR PA DON GNYER JI BZHIN MI SKYE ZHING,
,KUN 'BYUNG 'KHOR BA'I 'JUG RIM MA BSAMS NA,
,'KHOR BA'I RTZA BA GCOD TSUL MI SHES PAS,

> **If we don't make**
> **Sincere efforts**
> **In contemplating**

> **The problems of**
> **The truth of suffering,**

> **Then we won't be able**
> **To give birth**

> **To a truly authentic form**
> **Of the wish for freedom.**

And suppose
We are unable
To contemplate, properly,

The various stages
In which the circle
Starts to turn:

The source
Of suffering.

We will never
Understand how to sever
The very root of the cycle of pain.

[159]
'KHOR BA LAS THAR BAR 'DOD PAS THOG MAR SDUG KUN GNYIS KYI NYES DMIGS BSAM DGOS TE,

If we have any hopes of gaining freedom from the cycle of pain, then the first thing we have to do is to contemplate the problems of the two truths of suffering and its source.

[160]
NGAN SONG GSUM GYI SDUG BSNGAL DANG BDE 'GRO'I SDUG BSNGAL SPYI DANG BYE BRAG SKYE RGAN {%RGA NA} 'CHI SOGS **SDUG** BSNGAL **BDEN** PAS BSDUS PA'I 'KHOR BA'I **NYES DMIGS**

The *problems* of the cycle are all summarized in *the truth of suffering,* which covers in a general sense the sufferings of the three lower realms, and the sufferings of the higher realms. More specifically, these involve the pain of being born; of aging; of sickness, dying, and all the rest.

[161]
BSAM PA LA {%**LA MA**} '**BAD NA** NI, SDUG BSNGAL LAS THAR 'DOD MED PAR **THAR PA DON GNYER** GYI BLO **JI** LTA BA **BZHIN MI SKYE ZHING**,

If we don't make sincere efforts in contemplating these facts, then we will never feel any desire to gain freedom from suffering—which means *then* that *we won't be able to give birth,* in our hearts, *to a truly authentic form of the wish for freedom.*

[162]
'DOD CHAGS SOGS KYI NGO BO SKYE TSUL JI LTAR YIN PA'I KHYAD PAR SHES PA'I SGO NAS **KUN 'BYUNG** BDEN PA '**KHOR BA'I 'JUG RIM** TU 'GRO TSUL **MA BSAMS NA**,

And then *suppose* also that *we are unable to* understand the details of how the very essence of emotions like desire and the like arise inside of us—which then means we are incapable of *contemplating properly* the workings of *the various stages in which the circle starts to turn:* the mechanism of the truth of *the source of suffering.*

[163]
'BEN MA MTHONG BAR MDA' 'PHAN PA BZHIN '**KHOR BA'I RTZA BA GCOD TSUL MI SHES PAS** SO,,

In this case, *we will never understand how to sever the very root of the cycle of pain;* we will end up like an archer who shoots his arrow but without ever seeing the target.

Contemplating pain

[164]
GNYIS PA LA GNYIS, SDUG BSNGAL 'KHOR BA'I NYES DMIGS DANG, KUN 'BYUNG GI 'KHOR BA'I 'JUG RIM BSAM PA'O,,

Which brings us to that second topic: the actual method for engaging in this contemplation on the first two truths. Here we have two points: the contemplation of the problems of the cycle of pain, in the form of actual suffering; and then the contemplation of the problems of this cycle, in the form of the source of the suffering.

[165]
DANG PO NI, SRID LAS NGES 'BYUNG SOGS TE,

The first of these is expressed in the lines that include "a strong desire to escape from this life of pain":

[166]
(20a)
,SRID LAS NGES 'BYUNG SKYO SHAS BRTAN PA DANG,

> **We need to find**
> **Within ourselves**
>
> **Disgust and exhaustion**
> **With this situation:**
>
> **A strong desire**
> **To escape from**
> **This life of pain.**

[167]
'KHOR BA'I GNAS SU SKYE RGAN {%RGA NA} 'CHI BZHI DANG MYA NGAN DANG SMRE SNGAGS 'DON PA YID MI BDE BA DANG TSA GRANG 'THAB RTZOD [f. 7a] SOGS KYI SDUG BSNGAL RNAMS MTHONG NAS

Here in the land of the cycle of pain, we see the four of rebirth, aging, sickness, and dying; as well as grief, and crying out in pain; and the pains of unhappiness, excessive heat or cold, and conflict, and all the rest.

[168]
SRID PA 'KHOR BA **LAS NGES** PAR **'BYUNG** 'DOD KYI **SKYO SHAS**
DRAG PO **BSTEN PA DANG**, 'CHAD 'GYUR LTAR SDUG BSNGAL DE
BSKYED PA'I RGYU YANG SHES PAR BYA'O,,

As such, *we need to find within ourselves*[28] fierce feelings of
*disgust and exhaustion with this situation: a strong desire to
escape from this life of pain,* in the form of the cycle. We also
need to educate ourselves—as we will explain further
on—in the causes that create this suffering.

The problems of our cycle

[169]
GNYIS PA NI, 'KHOR BAR GANG GIS SOGS TE,

Which brings us to our second point here: the
contemplation of the problems of this cycle, in the form
of the source of the suffering. This is expressed in the
lines that include "what it is that keeps us chained to this
cycle of pain":

[170]

(20b)

,'KHOR BAR GANG GIS BCINGS PA SHES PA GCES,

---

[28] *Find within ourselves:* This phrase is how we have translated the Tibetan
verb *bsten-pa* here, which literally means "to rely upon" things like a
doctor or medicine. Many versions of the root text (such as our own,
here) spell this word here with a homonym: *brtan-pa.* This word would
indicate that our feelings of disgust and exhaustion with our current life
situation should be *very strong,* or *firm.*

A native Tibetan monastic would be remembering, in this section, the
list of the relationships we should have with the four truths: *understand*
the truth of suffering; *eliminate* the truth of its source; *bring about* the
cessation of suffering; and *practice* the path to this cessation. See for
example f. 7b of the *Jewel Necklace for Intelligent Young Minds* by Master
Kedrup Jinpa Dargye (b. 1558) (B14, S00208).

,RNAL 'BYOR NGAS KYANG NYAMS LEN DE LTAR BGYIS,
,THAR 'DOD KHYED KYANG DE BZHIN BSKYANG 'TSAL LO,

> We need to treasure
> The knowledge
>
> Of what it is
> That keeps us chained
> To this cycle of pain.
> I, the deep practitioner,
> Have accomplished my practice
> This way;
>
> And you who hope for freedom
> Should do your practice
> The same.

[171]
'KHOR BAR 'CHING BA {%'CHING} BYED **GANG GIS** BTZANGS BA
{%**BCINGS PA**} **SHES PA GCES** PA STE GAL CHE'O,,

We need to "treasure"—which is to say, it's crucial to
possess—*the knowledge of what it is that keeps us chained
to this cycle of pain:* we need to find out just what that is.

[172]
'CHING BYED LA LAS NYON GNYIS TE KHYAD PAR PHYEN {%PHYE
NA} MANG YANG, DON BSGRIL NA SO SKYE'I RGYUD KYI 'DOD
CHAGS KHONG KHRO NGA RGYAL MA RIG PA THE TSOM NYON
MONGS CAN PHRAG DOG SOGS NYON MONGS THAMS CAD NI

And what keeps us shackled here is the pair of our karma,
and our own negative emotions. Now there are many
ways of dividing up the details of these two, but to put it
all in a nutshell, we are talking first about all the negative
emotions that we find in the mindstream of a common

being:[29] ignorant desire; anger; pride; misunderstanding; unfounded doubts; jealousy; and so on.

[173]
NYON MONGS PA'I KUN 'BYUNG BDEN PA YIN LA, NYON MONGS DES KUN NAS BSLANGS PA'I LAS DGE MI DGE GANG YIN KYANG LAS KYI KUN 'BYUNG BDEN PA YIN NO,,

Collectively, these represent the truth of the source of suffering involved with negative emotions. And then any good or bad karma—action—inspired by these negative emotions represents the truth of the source of suffering involved with karma.

[174]
DE YANG GTZO BO MA RIG PA'I DBANG GIS LAS BSAGS LAS KYI DBANG GIS 'KHOR BAR 'JUG PA'I RTEN 'BREL YAN LAG BCU GNYIS KYI RIM PA LEGS PAR SHES SHING,

Now to really get a good grasp of how misunderstanding drives our accumulation of karma, and how karma spins the cycle of pain, we need a clear understanding of the various stages of the twelve links of how things occur in dependence upon each other.

[175]
MDOR NA LAS DANG NYON MONGS GNYIS KYI DBANG GIS 'KHOR BAR 'KHOR TSUL RNAMS BLA MA'I MAN NGAG LA BRTEN NAS SHES PA NI, KUN 'BYUNG 'KHOR BA'I 'JUG RIM SHES PA'O,,

To put it briefly, learning how it is that we spin in the cycle of pain through the power of the pair of our karma and negative emotions is something that we can learn by relying upon the personal advices of our Lama. This then

---

[29] *In the mindstream of a common being:* The expression "common being" is used to refer to a person who has not yet perceived emptiness directly.

is what we refer to as "understanding the truth of the source of suffering: the steps that make the cycle spin."

[176]
'KHOR BA'I RTZA BA GCOD TSUL NI BDAG MED RTOGS PA'I SHES RAB KYIS MA RIG PA'I ZHEN YUL LEGS PAR SUN PHYUNG BA'I TSUL GYIS

The way in which we sever the root of the cycle of pain is a process where the wisdom with which we grasp that nothing is itself serves to root out— perfectly—what our misunderstanding believes it sees.

[177]
GOMS PAR BYAS PA'I MTHAR MA RIG PA SPANGS PA NA 'KHOR BA'I RTZA BA BCAD CING, NYON MONGS GZHAN THAMS CAD KYANG ZHOR LA SBYONG BAR 'GYUR BA YIN NO,,

We then accustom ourselves to this process, and in the end we are able to eliminate our misunderstanding. When we reach this point, we have succeeded in severing the root of the cycle of pain; and then, with this, all of our other negative emotions are cleaned out, just by the way.

[178]
SDUG KUN GNYIS KYI NANG NAS BUN {%KUN} 'BYUNG SPANGS NA SHING RTZA BA BCAD NA BSKAMS 'GRO BA LTAR SDUG BSNGAL YANG SPONG
BAR 'GYUR PA GZHUNG CHEN PO RNAMS KYI DGONGS PA YIN MOD,

Suppose then that—from among the two truths of suffering and its source—we are able to eliminate the source. In this case we will also be able to eliminate the suffering, automatically: it's similar to the way in which a tree dries up, once we cut its roots. This is, admittedly, the intent of the major classics of Buddhism.

[179]
DENG SANG GI LAS DANG PO BAS NI, NYON MONGS RTZA BA
NAS SPONG MI NUS PAS, STOBS BZHI'I BSHAGS PA LA BRTEN NAS
KUN 'BYUNG GI NANG TSAN SDIG LTUNG RNAMS SPONG BA
GNAD CHE'O,,

Nowadays though those of us who are just starting
out are not going to be able to eliminate our negative
emotions from the very root. As such, it is crucial for
us to focus on using the practice of confession—through
the four powers—to eliminate the element of the truth of
the source of suffering represented by our bad deeds and
broken commitments.

[180]
KHYAD PAR DU TSUL KHRIMS KYI BSLAB PA SOGS GSUM LA 'BAD
DGOS LA, TSUL KHRIMS KYI BSLAB PA NI GTZO BO'I DBANG DU
BYAS NA MI DGE BA BCU SPONG BA'I SPONG SEMS YIN LA,

Most especially, we need to focus our efforts on the trio
that starts off with the training of following an ethical
lifestyle. What this particular training, of an ethical life,
primarily consists of is the decision to give up our bad
deeds: to stop doing the ten negative actions.[30]

[181]
TING NGE 'DZIN GYI BSLAB PA'I GTZO BO NI [f. 7b] ZHI GNAS YIN
MOD, DER MA NGES TE DGE BA'AM YANG DAG PA'I DMIGS PA

---

[30] *Ten negative actions:* These begin with three actions that we commit
physically: (1) taking life, (2) stealing others' things, and (3) sexual
misconduct—here, primarily referring to adultery with another person's
committed partner. Next are four bad deeds of speech: (4) lying; (5)
splitting up other people with things that we say; (6) harsh types of
speech; and (7) idle talk. Then finally are the three mental misdeeds of (8)
being unhappy when something good happens to someone else; (9) being
happy when something bad happens to them; and (10) wrong views
such as the belief that the laws of karma are mistaken, or that there is no
ultimate refuge.

LA RING THUD {%THUNG} GANG YIN YANG RTZE GCIG TU GNAS PA'I SEMS PA RNAMS TING NGE 'DZIN GYI BSLAB PAS BSDUS SO,,

As for the training in meditative concentration, the primary form is—admittedly—quietude. But it might also take other forms. Any time our thoughts are focused one-pointedly on something good, or pure—and no matter how long the particular period of focus may be—this is included into the training of meditative concentration.

[182]
SHES RAB KYI BSLAB PA'I GTZO BO NI LHAG MTHONG YIN KYANG, DER MA NGES TE, BDAG MED PHRA RAGS CI RIGS LA DPYOD PA'I RIGS PA DON MTHUN RNAMS DANG, CHOS KYI TSIG DON GZHAN LA'ANG LEGS PAR DPYOD PA'I SHES RAB RNAMS NI SHES RAB KYI BSLAB PAR 'DUS SO,,

It's similar with the training in wisdom; the primary form is, admittedly, special insight. But other forms are also possible. Accurate forms of logical thinking in which we perceive the fact that things are not themselves—in either the subtle or more gross forms of this fact—are also in included into this training; as are forms of wisdom where we examine, accurately, the meaning of Dharma teachings on other subjects.

The Wish as the basis

[183]
GSUM PA SKYES BU CHEN PO'I LAM GYI RIM PA LA GNYIS, SPYOD PA'I RTEN SEMS BSKYED DANG, SPYOD PA LA BSLAB TSUL LO,,

This brings us to our third section from above—the actual path for people of greater capacity. Here we have two parts: the Wish for enlightenment which is the basis for the activities of a bodhisattva; and then instructions for training ourselves in these activities.

[184]
DANG PO LA GNYIS LAS, DANG PO KHYAD CHOS SAM PHAN YON
NI, SEMS BSKYED THEG MCHOG SOGS BZHI STE,

The first of these has two sections of its own. The first of
these is a list of the features, or benefits, that we find here.
This is expressed in the four lines [of the Tibetan] which
include: "The Wish for enlightenment...the supreme
vehicle":

[185]
(21)
,SEMS BSKYED THEG MCHOG LAM GYI GZHUNG SHING STE,
,RLABS CHEN SPYOD PA RNAMS KYI GZHI DANG RTEN,
,TSOGS GNYIS KUN LA GSER 'GYUR RTZI LTA BU,
,RAB 'BYAMS DGE TSOGS SDUD PA'I BSOD NAMS GTER,

The Wish for enlightenment
Is the main beam
That holds up the entire path
Of the supreme vehicle.

It is the foundation,
And the basis,

For vastly effective
Activities.

For everything about
The two collections
Of merit & wisdom,

The Wish is like
That alchemical elixir
Which turns things
Into gold.

**It is a mine of merit
Which incorporates
Collections of
A myriad number
Of good deeds.**

[186]
THEG CHEN **SEMS BSKYED** NI, **THEG MCHOG** LAS KYI {%**LAM GYI**} **GZHUNG SHING** LTA BU **STE**, SBYIN DRUG SOGS **RLABS CHEN SPYOD PA RNAMS KYI** SKYE BA DANG GNAS PA DANG 'PHEL BA'I **GZHI DANG RTEN** YIN LA,

The Wish for enlightenment, as we find it in the greater way,[31] *is like the main beam that holds up the entire path of the supreme vehicle. It is the foundation, and the basis, for vastly effective activities* such as the six types of giving[32]—allowing them to start, to remain, and to flourish.

[187]
BSOD NAMS DANG YE SHES KYI **TSOGS GNYIS KUN** RDZOGS BYANG DU SGYUR BAR BYED PA **LA**, LCAGS KHAMS GSER DU SGYUR BAR BYED PA'I **GSER 'GYUR** GYI **RTZI LTA BU** DANG, **RAB 'BYAMS DGE TSOGS** MANG PO **SDUD PA'I BSOD NAMS** KYI **GTER** CHEN PO'O,,

What we seek to do is to transform *everything about the two collections of merit & wisdom* into total enlightenment. The Wish for enlightenment, in this context, is *like that*

---

[31] *As we find it in the greater way:* It might seem superfluous to refer to the Wish "as found in the greater way"; but technically there do exist, in some classical presentations, wishes for goals lower than complete enlightenment for the sake of every living being in the universe.

[32] *Six types of giving:* Not a terribly common division, but found in the *Jewel of the Shining Gem,* a commentary to the *Compendium of the Sutras* by Arya Nagarjuna, as giving which is (1) unconditional; (2) performed with joy; (3) repeated again & again; (4) presented to an appropriate recipient; (5) total; and (6) offered to ones followers. See f. 228a (S4, TD03935).

alchemical elixir which turns the element of iron *into gold* itself. *It is a great mine of merit which incorporates* a great many *collections of a myriad number of good deeds.*

[188]
GZHUNG 'DIS SEMS DE BSKYED DGOS PA'I RGYU MTSAN YANG BSTAN LA, GZHI DANG RTEN ZHES PAS THEG CHEN SEMS BSKYED DE, THEG CHEN LAM GYI 'JUG SGOR YANG BSTAN TO,,

These particular lines are also intended to convey to us the reasons why we really need to develop this Wish for enlightenment within ourselves. They are further meant to convey, in the phrase "foundation & basis," that the Wish is the door that we need to use, to enter the path to the greater way.

The method for developing the Wish

[189]
GNYIS PA BSKYED TSUL NI, DE LTAR SHES NAS SOGS GNYIS TE,

This brings us to our second section here, which is the method that we need to use to develop this Wish within us. That topic is conveyed in the two lines [of the Tibetan] which include "Once they have learned thus":

[190]
(22)
,DE LTAR SHES NAS RGYAL SRAS DPA' BO RNAMS,
,RIN CHEN SEMS MCHOG THUGS DAM MTHIL DU 'DZIN,
,RNAL 'BYOR NGAS KYANG NYAMS LEN DE LTAR BGYIS,
,THAR 'DOD KHYED KYANG DE BZHIN BSKYANG 'TSAL LO,

**Once they have
Learned thus,**

The children of the Victors—
The warriors—

Make this supreme
State of mind,
This jewel,

The spiritual centerpiece
Of their practice.

I, the deep practitioner,
Have accomplished my practice
This way;

And you who hope for freedom
Should do your practice
The same.

[191]
THEG CHEN SEMS BSKYED KYI KHYAD CHOS SAM PHAN YON
DE LTAR SHES NAS RGYAL BA'I **SRAS** BYANG CHUB SEMS DPA'
GZHAN DON DU 'JUG PAR NUS PA **DPA' BO RNAMS** KYIS NI,

Once they have learned thus the features or benefits of the
Wish for enlightenment in the greater way, there is a
certain way of proceeding for *warriors*—which is to say,
for these bodhisattvas, or *children of the Victors*, able as
they are to engage in acting for the sake of others.

[192]
SEMS CAN THAMS CAD KYI DON DU SANGS RGYAS THOB 'DOD
KYI **RIN CEN SEMS MCHOG** DE NYAMS YON {%LEN} GYI GTZO
BO'AM **THUGS DAM** GYI **MTHIL DU 'DZIN** PAR MDZAD PA LTAR
BYA'O,,

What these warriors do is that they *make this supreme state of mind, this jewel*[33] — the desire to reach enlightenment for the sake of each & every living being — the primary element or *spiritual centerpiece of their practice*. And we are meant to do the same.

[193]
RJE BTZUN SOGS SNGAR BZHIN NO,,

Once again, the lines about "the holy Lamas" and so forth should be read as we have covered them previously here.

The fine qualities of giving

[194]
GNYIS PA SPYOD PA LA BSLAB TSUL LA DRUG ,SBYIN PA, TSUL KHRIMS, BZOD PA, BRTZON 'GRUS, BSAM GTAN, SHES RAB PO,,

Which brings us to our second part from above: instructions for training ourselves in these activities. Here we have six divisions: giving, the ethical life, patience, joyful effort, meditation, and wisdom.

[195]
DANG PO LA GNYIS LAS DANG PO KHYAD CHOS SAM PHAN YON NI, SBYIN PA 'GRO BA'I SOGS BZHI STE,

The first of these has two topics of its own. The first of these is a listing of the features, or benefits, and is expressed in the four lines [of the Tibetan] which read, "Giving, for living beings":

---

[33] *This jewel:* The Tibetan for this word in the carving we are using is spelled *rin-cen,* which is a rare but acceptable variant for the nearly ubiquitous *rin-chen.*

[196]

(23)

,SBYIN PA 'GRO BA'I RE SKONG YID BZHIN NOR,
,SER SNA'I MDUD PA GCOD PA'I MTSON CHA MCHOG
,MA ZHUM SNYING STOBS BSKYED PA'I RGYAL SRAS SPYOD,
,SNYAN PA'I GRAGS PA PHYOGS BCUR SGROG PA'I GZHI,

Giving is a wishing jewel
Which fulfils the hopes
Of living beings;

It is a supreme blade
For cutting
The knot of stinginess.
It is an activity
For children of the Victors
Which inspires within us

A kind of courage,
Where we are never
Hesitant;

And it serves as a basis
For the praises
Of our fame

To be proclaimed
In all the ten directions.

[197]
[f. 8a] LUS LONGS SPYOD SOGS GZHAN LA GTONG BA'I **SBYIN PA**
NI, SLONG BA PO'I **'GRO BA'I RE** BA **SKONG** BAR BYED PA'I **YID
BZHIN** GYI **NOR** BU LTA BU DANG,

The perfection of *giving*—where we give away things
like our own body, or our possessions, to others—*is* like
a wishing jewel which functions to *fulfil the hopes of* those
living beings who are asking for things.

[198]
DNGOS PO LA CHAGS ZHEN GCOD PA'I PHYIR NA **SER SNA'I MDUD PA GCOD PA'I MTSON CHA MCHOG** YIN LA,

This perfection is also *a supreme blade for cutting the knot of stinginess,* for it severs our habitual attachment to the things we possess.

[199]
'GRO BA'I DON LA **MA ZHUM** ZHING **SNYING STOBS SKYED PA'I RGYAL SRAS** KYI **SPYOD** PA DANG,

This *is* also *a* particular *activity for children of the Victors which inspires within us a kind of courage, where we are never hesitant* to undertake actions that will be of help to other living beings.

[200]
GTONG BA PO'I **SNYAN PA'I GRAGS PA PHYOGS BCUR SGROGS PA'I GZHI'O,,**

And then finally, this perfection *serves as a basis for* the *praises of* the giver's *fame to be proclaimed in all the ten directions* of the world.

How we do our giving

[201]
GNYIS PA GTONG TSUL NI, DE LTAR SHES NAS SOGS,

Our second topic here is the method in which we do our giving. This is expressed in the lines that include "Once they understand how all this works":

[202]

(24)
,DE LTAR SHES NAS LUS DANG LONGS SPYOD DGE

,YONGS SU GTONG BA'I LAM BZANG MKHAS PAS BSTEN,
,RNAL 'BYOR NGAS KYANG NYAMS LEN DE LTAR BGYIS,
,THAR 'DOD KHYED KYANG DE BZHIN BSKYANG 'TSAL LO,

Once they understand
How all this works,
Wise ones betake themselves
To this noble path,

Where they feel free
To give away their body,
The things that they possess,
And their goodness.

I, the deep practitioner,
Have accomplished my practice
This way;

And you who hope for freedom
Should do your practice
The same.

[203]
TSUL **DE LTAR SHES NAS** RANG GI **LUS DANG** ZAS NOR SOGS **LONGS SPYOD** DANG, BDER GE {%BDE **DGE**} THAMS CAD GZHAN LA **YONGS SU GTONG BA'I LAM BZANG** PO **MKHAS PAS BSTEN** PAR BYA'O,,

Once they understand how all this works, then *wise ones betake themselves to this noble path, where they feel free to give away*—to everyone else—everything: *their own body;* other *things that they possess,* such as food or money; *and* all *their* happiness & *goodness.*

[204]
LONGS SPYOD ZHES PAS ZANG ZING GI SBYIN PA DANG, DGE ZHES PAS KYANG CHOS KYI SBYIN PA'ANG BSDUS SHING, MI 'JIGS SBYIN PA NI SHUGS KYIS THOB PO,,

When the lines say "things they possess" here, it is meant to cover the practice of giving away material objects. Then when it says "goodness," this is meant to include as well the gift of the Dharma. And then this includes, by implication, giving others freedom from fear.[34]

The fine qualities
of an ethical life

[205]
GNYIS PA LA SNGAR LTAR GNYIS LAS, DANG PO NI, TSUL KHRIMS NYES SPYOD SOGS BZHI STE,

As for our second perfection here—following an ethical life—we will proceed in the same two topics.[35] The first of them is expressed in the lines that include, "The practice of leading an ethical life washes away all bad behavior":

[206]
(25)
,TSUL KHRIMS NYES SPYOD DRI MA 'KHRUD PA'I CHU,
,NYON MONGS TSA GDUNG SEL BA'I ZLA BA'I 'OD,
,SKYE DGU'I DBUS NA LHUN PO LTA BUR BRJID,
,STOBS KYIS BSDIGS PA MED PAR 'GRO KUN 'DUD,

The practice of leading
An ethical life

Is pure water
Which washes away

---

[34] Freedom from fear: This section is an indirect allusion to specific vows within the practice of advanced Buddhism, or the Diamond Way. Here, within the pledges of the "family" of the high Buddha known as the "Jewels," we commit to four different forms of generosity: giving material things; giving protection; giving the Dharma; and giving love.

[35] *Same two topics*: That is, first listing the fine qualities of the perfection, and then how to practice it.

The stains of all
Bad behavior.

It is moonlight
That clears away
The torment of the heat
Of negative emotions.

It stands with majesty
Among the crowds
Of humankind,
Like the central mountain.

Due to its power,
All beings bow down,
And never think
To threaten us.

[207]
TSUL KHRIMS LA NYES SPYOD SDOM PA, DGE BA CHOS SDUD{%,}
SEMS CAN DON BYED GSUM LAS GTZO BOR NYES SPYOD SDOM
PA'I DBANG DU BYAS NA, TSUL KHRIMS DE NI, SGO GSUM GYI
NYES SPYOD KYI **DRI MA 'KHRUD PA'I CHU** LTA BU DANG,

Now generally, *the practice of* leading *an ethical life* can
be divided into the three of restraining ourselves from
negative behavior; gathering in good deeds; and carrying
out the needs of suffering living beings. The lines here
are focusing primarily on the first of these. And what
we can say about this particular observance of an ethical
lifestyle is that it is similar to *pure water which washes away
the stains of all bad behavior* committed through any of the
three doors of actions, words, or thoughts.

[208]
NYON MONGS PA'I **TSA GDUNG SEL BA**R BYED PA'I **ZLA BA'I**

'OD LTA BU DANG,

It is, as well, like *moonlight that clears away the torment of the heat of* everything involved with the *negative emotions.*[36]

[209]
SRUNG BA PO'I RTEN GYI GANG ZAG DE **SKYE RGU'I DBUS NA** BI {%RI} RGYAL **LHUN PO LTA BUR BRJID** CHE ZHING,

Further, someone who is the type of person who carefully guards their morality *stands with majesty among the crowds of humankind*—something *like the central mountain* of the entire world.[37]

[210]
DE LTA BU'I **STOBS KYIS** GZHAN DAG GIS RANG LA 'TSE BA'I **BSDIGS PA MED PAR 'GRO** BA KUN 'DUD PAR BYED DO,,

And *due to* the *power* of this majesty, *all beings bow down to* the truly ethical individual, *and* no one else would *ever think to threaten* or harm *us* then, in any way.

How to follow an ethical life

[211]
GNYIS PA SRUNG TSUL NI, DE LTAR SHES NAS SOGS TE,

Our second topic then is how to actually follow the

---

[36] *Clears away the torment of the heat:* In the traditional sources, rays of sunlight are described as functioning to ripen crops; while rays of moonlight serve to provide coolness to counteract excessive heat

[37] *Central mountain of the world:* Buddhist cosmology sees our planet as a flat disk with an incredibly high mountain at the center.

perfection of an ethical life. This is expressed in the lines that include "once we understand all this":

[212]

(26)

,DE LTAR SHES NAS YANG DAG BLANGS PA'I KHRIMS,
,DAM PA RNAMS KYIS MIG BZHIN BSRUNG BAR MDZAD,
,RNAL 'BYOR NGAS KYANG NYAMS LEN DE LTAR BGYIS,
,THAR 'DOD KHYED KYANG DE BZHIN BSKYANG 'TSAL LO,

> Once we understand all this,
> We need to act
> As the holy ones did,
>
> Protecting the practice
> Of a truly pure,
> Ethical life
>
> In the same way
> That we instinctively
> Shield our eyes.
>
> I, the deep practitioner,
> Have accomplished my practice
> This way;
>
> And you who hope for freedom
> Should do your practice
> The same.

[213]

TSUL **DE LTAR SHES NAS YANG DAG** PAR **BLANGS PA'I** TSUL **KHRIMS** NI SNGON GYI **DAM PA RNAMS KYIS MIG BZHIN** DU SRUNG **BAR MDZAD** PA LTAR BYA'O,,

Once we understand how *all this* works, we need to follow the example of *holy ones* of the past, *acting as they did.* They considered *the practice of a truly pure, ethical life* to be something which we should assiduously *protect, in*

the same way that we all *instinctively shield our eyes* from something that might poke them.

The fine qualities of patience

[214]
GSUM PA LA GNYIS LAS DANG PO NI, BZOD PA STOBS LDAN SOGS BZHI STE,

With this we have reached our third perfection, which we will cover in the same two topics. Here we start off from the four lines [of the Tibetan] which include "Patience... for those of true strength":

[215]
(27)
,BZOD PA STOBS LDAN RNAMS LA RGYAN GYI MCHOG
,[f. 57a] NYON MONGS GDUNG BA'I DKA' THUB KUN GYI PHUL,
,ZHE SDANG LAG 'GRO'I DGRA LA NAM MKHA' LDING,
,TSIG RTZUB MTSON LA SRA BA'I GO CHA YIN,

> Patience is the highest jewel
> For those of true strength;
>
> It is the very acme,
> Or highest asceticism
> Of all, for those
> Tormented by
> Negative emotions.
>
> It is a skyglider
> Against the enemy
>
> Of the palm walker
> Of anger.
>
> And it is
> Impenetrable armor
> Against the

Spears & arrows
Of harsh words.

[216]
BZOD PA LA SDUG BSNGAL DANG YIN {%LEN}, GNOD PA LA JI MI
SNYAM PA, CHOS LA NGES THOB KYI BZOD PA GSUM LAS, 'DIR
DNGOS BSTAN PAR BA'I DBANG DU BYAS NAS GNOD PA LA BZOD
PA'I BZOD PA NI,

Now the perfection of *patience* can be divided into three
different types: willingly taking on pains; letting go of
harm done to us; and hardships undertaken to master
the Dharma. The kind of patience directly indicated
in the verse here is the kind where we learn to bear up
under harm which others do us.

[217]
GNOD PA'I KHUR SKYER NUS PA'I BYANG SEMS **STOBS LDAN
RNAMS LA** MDZES [f. 8b] BYED DU GYUR PA'I **RGYAN GYI MCHOG**
YIN LA,

This patience is the *highest jewel* that bodhisattvas of
true strength—those who are able to carry the heavy
burden of what others have done to hurt them—
wear upon their person, and which lends them a
true beauty.

[218]
NYON MONGS PA'I MES **GDUNG BA'I** GNYEN PO LA DKA'
THUB DU MA YOD KYANG, **DKA' THUB KUN GYI PHUL** TE
MCHOG DANG

And we can further say that—despite the fact that there
are a great many difficult spiritual practices that we can
undertake as counteragents to being *tormented by* the fire
of everything involved with the *negative emotions*—this
patience is *the very acme, or highest asceticism of all.*

[219]
ZHE SDANG LAG 'GRO STE SPRUL {%SBRUL} GYIS {%GYIS MTSON PAR} BYED PA SLU'I {%KLU'I} **DGRA LA** MANG DU YOD KYANG, **NAM MKHA'I LDING** STE KHYUD {%KHYUNG} BZHIN DANG,

So too we can say that *the "palm walker"*—or snake (which is a metaphor being used for *anger* here); or else we can also say "dragon"—has many different kinds of *enemies.* But its most powerful foe is the *skyglider,* of forbearance.[38]

[220]
PHA ROL GYIS **TSIG RTZUB** KYI **MTSON** 'PHEN PA **LA** DES MI MIG {%PHIGS} PA'I **SRA BA'I GO CHA** SRAB {%KHRAB} LTA BU **YIN** NO,,

Patience is, finally, very much like *impenetrable armor against the spears & arrows of* the *harsh words* that other people might say to us, proof against being impaled by their sharp points.

How to keep your patience

[221]
GNYIS PA DE BSGOM PA NI, DE LTAR SHES NAS SOGS TE,

Which brings us to our second point here, on how to keep our patience. This is found in the words of the root text which include "Once they realized this":

---

[38] *Skyglider of forbearance:* Traditional Sanskrit, and Tibetan, poetics features vivid, made-up words as sort of riddles, to represent different objects and beings in the world. Here "palm walker" (in Sanskrit, *bhujaṅga*) refers to a snake, since it slides on its flat belly. And then "skyglider" (in Tibetan, *nam-mkha' lding*) connotes the *garuda,* a powerful mythical eagle much like the western phoenix, and which delights in carrying off snakes and eating them in mid-air. Your translators have observed this in person with the American eagle and rattlesnake, in the Arizona desert.

[222]

(28)
,DE LTAR SHES NAS BZOD MCHOG GO CHA LA,
,RNAM PA SNA TSOGS TSUL GYIS GOMS PAR MDZAD,
,RNAL 'BYOR NGAS KYANG NYAMS LEN DE LTAR BGYIS,
,THAR 'DOD KHYED KYANG DE BZHIN BSKYANG 'TSAL LO,

Once they realized this,
They undertook to
Accustom their hearts—

In a great variety
Of different ways—

To donning
Their own armor:
A supreme form
Of patience.

I, the deep practitioner,
Have accomplished my practice
This way;

And you who hope for freedom
Should do your practice
The same.

[223]

TSUL **DE LTAR SHES NAS BZOD** PA'I **MCHOG** SNGON GYI DAM
PAS RANG GI **GO CHA LA** THABS **RNAMS SNA TSOGS TSUL GYIS**
RGYUD LA **GOMS PAR MDZAD** PA LTAR BYA'O,,

Once they realized how all *this* works, holy ones of the
past *undertook to accustom their hearts—in a great variety of
different ways—to* this method of *donning their own armor:
a supreme form of patience.* We too must learn to do the
same.

The fine qualities
of joyful effort

[224]

BZHI PA LA GNYIS LAS, DANG PO NI, BRTZON 'GRUS LA GSUM
LAS, DANG PO NI, MI BZLOG BRTAN PA'I SOGS BZHI STE,

This brings us to our fourth perfection, which again has
those same two points. The first of these is described in
the words "steadfast...never turning back," which are
describing the first of the three different types of joyful
effort.[39]

[225]

(29)

,MI LDOG BRTAN PA'I BRTZON 'GRUS GO BGOS NA,
,LUNG RTOGS YON TAN YAR NGO'I ZLA BZHIN 'PHEL,
,SPYOD LAM THAMS CAD DON DANG LDAN PAR 'GYUR,
,GANG BRTZAMS LAS KYI MTHA' RNAMS YID BZHIN 'GRUB,

> Suppose we are able
> To don the strong armor
> Of steadfast, joyful effort,
> Never turning back.
>
> Our fine qualities—
> In both scriptural study
> And inner realizations—
> Will multiply,
> Like a waxing moon.
> Any project we undertake

---

[39] *Three types of joyful effort:* These three are the following. First we have
the "armor-like" effort that we see here, where we are iron-plated in our
determination to help all other beings. Then there is "joyful effort in the
accumulation of goodness," which is a joy in undertaking all the practices
of the Dharma. And then finally we have "joyful effort in accomplishing
the needs of others," which includes for example the different traditional
methods for attracting and serving our own disciples. For a great
description, see as usual that of the great Pabongka Rinpoche and Trijang
Rinpoche in *A Gift of Liberation,* starting from f. 344a (B12, S00004).

Will end up having
A meaningful result;

And any undertaking
We ever initiate
Will come to its

Successful conclusion,
Just as we intended.

[226]
GTZO BOR GO CHA'I BRTZON 'GRUS KYI DBANG DU BYAS NA,
PHYIR **MI BZLOG** CING **BRTAN PA'I BRTZON 'GRUS** KYI **GO** CHA
BGOS NA, **LUNG** DANG **RTOGS** PA'I **YON TAN** THAMS CAD **YAR**
DO'I {%**NGO'I**} **ZLA** BA **BZHIN** GONG DU **'PHEL** LA,

Focusing then primarily on the type of joyful effort called
"armor-like," *suppose* that *we are able to don the strong
armor of steadfast, joyful effort:* a kind of effort where we
never turn back.[40] In this case, all of *our fine qualities—in
both scriptural study and inner realizations—will multiply
ever more strongly, much *like a waxing moon.*

[227]
SPYOD LAM THAMS CAD LA RTZOM PA **DON DANG LDAN PAR
'GYUR** ZHING,

So too, *any project we undertake* in any of our various
activities *will end up having a meaningful result.*

[228]
RANG GIS BYA BA **GANG BRTZAMS** PA'I **LAS KYI MTHA' RNAMS
YID** LA BSAMS PA **BZHIN** DU **'GRUB** PAR 'GYUR RO,,

---

[40]   *Never turn back:* The spelling for this expression found in the
commentary—*mi bzlog*—is an acceptable variant, and homonym
(including the prenasal of the second syllable), for the spelling of the root
text: *mi ldog.*

And, finally, *any undertaking* that *we ever initiate will come to its intended, successful conclusion—just as we* originally hoped it would.

How to undertake joyful effort

[229]

GNYIS PA RTZOM TSUL NI, DE LTAR SHES NAS SOGS TE,

This brings us to the second point here, on how to undertake joyful effort. This is covered in the lines of the root text which include "they understood perfectly":

[230]

(30)
,DE LTAR SHES NAS LE LO KUN SEL BA'I,
,RLABS CHEN BRTZON 'GRUS RGYAL SRAS
RNAMS KYIS BRTZAMS,
,RNAL 'BYOR NGAS KYANG NYAMS LEN DE LTAR BGYIS,
,THAR 'DOD KHYED KYANG DE BZHIN BSKYANG 'TSAL LO,

> Children of the Victors
> Understood perfectly
> These points,
>
> And so they were
> Able to undertake
> Joyful effort which was
> Hugely effective,
>
> To clear away
> Every trace
> Of laziness.
>
> I, the deep practitioner,
> Have accomplished my practice

This way;

And you who hope for freedom
Should do your practice
The same.

[231]
JI SKAD BSHAD PA **DE LTAR SHES NAS** BYI {%PHYI} BSHOL GYI **LE LO KUN SEL BA**R BYED PA'**I RLABS CHEN** GYI **BRTZON 'GRUS** SNGON **RGYAL SRAS RNAMS KYIS BRTZAMS** PAR BYAS PA LTAR 'JUG GO

Children of the Victors who lived in days gone by *understood perfectly the points* being made here, *and so they were able to undertake* just this kind of *joyful effort:* one *which was hugely effective,* and which functioned to *clear away every trace of* the kind of *laziness* where we tend to procrastinate about things we're supposed to get done. We too then must do the same.

The fine qualities of meditation

[232]
,LNGA PA LA GNYIS LAS, DANG PO NI, BSAM GTAN SEMS LA SOGS BZHI STE,

This brings us, fifth, to the perfection of meditation, covered in those same two points. The first of them is expressed in the lines which include "meditation...over the mind":

[233]

(31)
,BSAM GTAN SEMS LA DBANG BSGYUR RGYAL PO STE,
,BZHAG NA G-YO MED RI YI DBANG PO BZHIN,
,BTANG NA DGE BA'I DMIGS PA KUN LA 'JUG
,LUS SEMS LAS SU RUNG BA'I BDE CHEN 'DREN,

Meditation is a king

Who enjoys total authority

Over the realm
Of their own mind.

When you place it
Upon an object,
It stays there

Completely immobile,
Like the king
Of all mountains.

And any time
You release this,
It moves off to
Every different kind
Of virtuous focus.

It always elicits
The great bliss
Where both body & mind
Are extremely flexible.

[234]
DMIGS PA RTZA {%RTZE} GCIG PA'I **BSAM GTAN** NI, RANG GI
SEMS LA JI LTAR 'DOD PA BZHIN **DBANG BSGYUR** BA'I **RGYAL PO**
LTA BHA {%BU} **STE**,

Meditation which is able to stay single-pointedly on its
object of focus can be compared to *a king, who enjoys total
authority over* their *realm;* in this case, over how *their mind*
behaves.

[235]
DE YANG DMIGS PA LA **BZHAG NA** NI, BYING RGOD KYIS **G-YO** BA
MED PAR DE {%RI} **YI DBANG PO** BZHIN DU GNAS LA,

Which is to say, *when you place* this kind of meditation *upon a* certain *object, it stays there completely immobile, like the king of all mountains*[41]—for it is unmoved by the pair of mental dullness or agitation.

[236]
BZHAG PA DE **BTANG NA** YANG **DGE BA'I DMIGS PA** STE YUL **KUN LA 'JUG** CING,

And any time we *release* this state of mind—after having placed it on a certain object—*it* invariably *moves off to every different kind of virtuous focus,* or object.

[237]
RANG GI **LUS SEMS** DGE BA'I PHYOGS LA BGOL TU RUNG BA'I **LAS SU RUNG BA'I** SHIN SBYANGS KYI **BDE CHEN 'DREN** NO,,

And then *it always elicits the great bliss* that comes from that mental litheness *where both* our *body and* our *mind are extremely flexible,* or easily directed towards things which are virtuous to do.

[238]
DMIGS PA LA RTZE GCIG TU BZHAG PA'I STOBS KYIS, LUS SEMS SHIN SBYANGS KYI BDE BA KHYAD PAR CAN 'DREN [f. 9a] TSUL NI RJE'I LAM RIM LAS SHES PAR BYA'O,,

If you would like more detail about how we elicit the bliss of an extraordinary degree of physical and mental flexibility by force of placing our mind single-pointedly on a particular object of focus, you can refer to the Lord's *Steps on the Path.*[42]

---

[41] *King of all mountains:* Again, referring to that highest central mountain of our disk-like planet.

[42] *The Lord's "Steps on the Path":* Here referring to Je Tsongkapa's *Great Book on the Steps of the Path to Enlightenment* (the *Lam Rim Chenmo*); see the

How to meditate

[239]
GNYIS PA BSGOM TSUL NI, DE LTAR SHES NAS SOGS TE,

Which brings us to our second point here: how to meditate. This topic is covered in the lines that include "armed with this understanding":

[240]
(32)
,DE LTAR SHES NAS RNAL 'BYOR DBANG PO RNAMS,
,RNAM G-YENG DGRA 'JOMS TING 'DZIN RGYUN DU BSTEN,
,RNAL 'BYOR NGAS KYANG NYAMS LEN DE LTAR BGYIS,
,THAR 'DOD KHYED KYANG DE BZHIN BSKYANG 'TSAL LO,

> Armed with this understanding,
> Lords among deep practitioners
> Undertook the constant practice
> Of focused meditation,
>
> Where they destroyed
> The enemy of distraction.
>
> I, the deep practitioner,
> Have accomplished my practice
> This way;
>
> And you who hope for freedom
> Should do your practice
> The same.

[241]
TSUL **DE LTAR SHES NAS** SNGON BYON PA'I **RNAL 'BYOR** GYI
DBANG PO RNAMS KYIS **RNAM G-YENG** GI **DGRA 'JOMS** SHING,
DMIGS PA LA RTZE GCIG PA'I **TING** NGE **'DZIN** DUS **RGYUN** TU
BSTEN PA LTAR BSLAB PO,,

---

extremely detailed section beginning at f. 305b (B8, S05392L).

Armed with an *understanding* of how all this works, those *lords among deep practitioners* who lived in days gone by *undertook the constant practice of focused meditation, where they* remained single-pointed upon the object, and *destroyed the enemy of distraction.* We too need to train ourselves in the same.

[242]
'DI NI GTZO BO ZHIG {%ZHI} GNAS BSGOMS PA'I DBANG DU BYAS LA, RJE BTZUN SOGS SNGAR BZHIN NO,,

This section by the way is referring primarily to the deep practice of meditation that we call "quietude." And then this would again be followed by the lines that include "the holy Lamas."

The fine qualities of wisdom

[243]
DRUG PA LA GSUM, SHES RAB BSGOM TSUL, ZHI LHAG ZUNG DU 'BREL TSUL, MNYAM RJES GNYIS KA SKYONG TSUL YAN LAG DANG BCAS PA'O,,

This then brings us to the sixth and final perfection, which is wisdom. We cover this topic in three different sections: how to meditate upon wisdom; how to combine quietude & special insight into a single unit; and then how to conduct both periods of a session—both balanced meditation and the aftermath period, along with some ancillary points.

[244]
DANG PO LA KHYAD CHOS SAM PHAN YON DANG, BSGOM TSUL GNYIS LAS, DANG PO NI, SHES RAB ZAB MO'I DE NYID SOGS BZHI STE,

We'll treat the first of these, again, in two parts of features, or benefits, and then move on to how we perform this particular meditation. The first of these is expressed in the four lines [of the Tibetan] which include "wisdom… to view profound suchness":

[245]

(33)
,SHES RAB ZAB MO'I DE NYID LTA BA'I MIG
,SRID PA'I RTZA BA DRUNGS NAS 'BYIN PA'I LAM,
,GSUNG RAB KUN LAS BSNGAGS PA'I YON TAN GTER,
,GTI MUG MUN SEL SGRON ME'I MCHOG TU GRAGS,

Wisdom is like
A pair of eyes
That allow us to view
Profound suchness.

It is a path
That enables us
To rip out the very root
Of this kind of life.

It is a great goldmine
Of all the fine
Personal qualities
So highly praised
In all of that highest
Of the spoken word.

It is renowned
As the supreme lamp,
Lighting up the darkness
Of our blind ignorance.

[246]
SHES RAB LA JI LTA BA RTOGS PA'I SHES RAB SOGS GSUM YOD
KYANG, 'DIR GTZO BO NI DANG PO'I DBANG DU BYAS NAS, ZAB

DON RTOGS PA'I **SHES RAB** NI,

Now in general, there are three different types of wisdom—such as "the wisdom with which we realize just how things are."[43] Here we are primarily referring to the *wisdom* with which we realize the profound reality.

[247]
CHOS RNAMS KYI **ZAB MO'I DE** KHO NA **NYID LTA BA**R BYED PA'I **MIG** LTA BU DANG,

This particular wisdom is *like a pair of eyes that allow us to view* the *profound suchness* of all existing entities.

[248]
SRID PA 'KHOR BA'**I RTZA BA** MA RIG PA **DRUNG NAS 'BYIN PA'I LAM** DU 'GYUR ZHING,

It is, as well, *a path that enables us to rip out* that misunderstanding which is *the very root of "this kind of life"*—referring to the cycle of pain.

[249]
YUM GYI MDO SOGS RGYAL BA'I **GSUNG RAB KUN LAS BSNGAGS PA'I YON TAN** GYI **GTER** CHEN PO DANG,

So too, this wisdom is *a* great *goldmine of all the fine personal qualities so highly praised in all of that highest of the spoken word:* the teachings of the Victors, such as the Mother Sutras.

---

[43] *Just how things are:* These three are listed for example by the great textbook writer of the glorious Sera Mey Tibetan Monastery, Kedrup Tenpa Dargye (1493-1568), as the wisdom with which we realize just how things are; the wisdom with which we perceive all the things there are; and the wisdom that accomplishes the needs of all living beings. See f. 127b of the first volume of his *Jewel of the Essence of Good Explanation* (B11, S00009-1).

[250]
RMONGS PA'I **GTI MUG** GI **MUN** PA **SEL** BAR BYED PA'I **SGRON ME MCHOG TU GRAGS** PA YIN NO,,

And then finally *it is renowned as the supreme lamp, lighting up the darkness of our blind ignorance* and misunderstanding.

How to meditate on wisdom

[251]
GNYIS PA NI, DE LTAR SHES NAS SOGS TE,

Which brings us to our second point here, on how to perform this meditation on wisdom. This is covered in the wording of the root text which includes "once they understand all this":

[252]

(34)

,DE LTAR SHES NAS THAR 'DOD MKHAS PA YIS,
,LAM DE 'BAD PA DU MAS BSKYED PAR MDZAD,
,RNAL 'BYOR NGAS KYANG NYAMS LEN DE LTAR BGYIS,
,THAR 'DOD KHYED KYANG DE BZHIN BSKYANG 'TSAL LO,

Once they understand all this,
Wise ones who seek for freedom
Make a great many efforts
In this path, undertaking
To produce it.

I, the deep practitioner,
Have accomplished my practice
This way;

And you who hope for freedom
Should do your practice
The same.

124

[253]
TSUL **DE LTAR SHES NAS THAR** PA 'DOD PA'I **MKHAS PA YIS
LAM DE** NYID '**BAD PA DU MAS** RANG RGYUD LA **BSKYED PAR
MDZAD** DO,,

Once they understand how *all this* works, then *wise ones who
seek for freedom make a great many efforts in this* very *path,
undertaking to produce it* within their own mindstream.

[254]
GONG DU BRJOD PA'I PHYIN DRUG SO SO'I NGO BO, DBYE BA
SOGS RGYAS PAR NI 'DIR MANG DU DOGS PAS

I have hesitated to present here what might be too much
information, in our present context, about the details
of these six perfections we've been describing; that is,
additional information about the essential nature of each
perfection; its more detailed divisions; and so on.

[255]
LAM RIM CHEN MO SOGS LAS SHES PAR BYA ZHING, DON BSDUS
PA ZHIG KHO BOS LAM RIM DMAR 'KHRID DU BSHAD ZIN TO,,

If though you would like to learn more, I encourage you
to refer to works like *The Great Book on the Steps of the Path.*
I have also already made a more concise presentation in
my own *Dissection Teaching on the Steps of the Path.*[44]

---

[44] *Dissection Teaching:* A "dissection teaching" refers to a commentarial
style where the author points out concepts and practices as vividly as a
medical instructor might lead their student doctors through the organs
of an actual corpse laying on a table. For details of the work mentioned,
see B2, S25235.

Why we need
quietude + insight

[256]
GNYIS PA LA GNYIS LAS, ZHI LHAG ZUNG 'BRAL {%'BREL} BSGOM
PA'I DGOS PA DANG, BSGOM TSUL DNGOS SO,,

With this, we have reached our second point here—how to combine quietude & special insight into a single unit. We'll present this topic in two parts: an explanation of why we need to meditate upon quietude and special insight combined into a single unit; and then the actual instructions for this particular type of meditation.

[257]
DANG PO NI, RTZE GCIG BSAM GTAN SOGS BRGYAD DE,

The first of these is expressed in the eight lines [of the Tibetan] which include "single-pointed meditation":[45]

[258]

(35)
,RTZE GCIG BSAM GTAN TZAM LA 'KHOR BA YI,
,RTZA BA GCOD PA'I NUS PA MA MTHONG ZHING,
,ZHI GNAS LAM DANG BRAL BA'I SHES RAB KYIS,
,JI TZAM DPYAD KYANG NYON MONGS MI LDOG PAS,

We can't see that
Single-pointed meditation
Would possess, by itself,

Sufficient power
To sever the root
Of the cycle of pain.

---

[45] *Eight lines of the Tibetan:* It would appear that there are actually ten lines of relevant text here, even excluding the usual refrain.

We can use wisdom
Divorced from the path
Of quietude to perform as much
Examination as we want,

But still we will find ourselves
Unable to put a stop
To our negative emotions.

[259]

(36)
,YIN LUGS PHU THAG CHOD PA'I SHES RAB DE,
,G-YO MED ZHI GNAS RTA LA BSKYON NAS NI,
,MTHA' [f. 57b] BRAL DBU MA'I RIGS PA'I MTSON RNON GYIS,
,MTHAR 'DZIN DMIGS GTOD {%GTAD} THAMS CAD 'JIG BYED
PA'I,

They took a form of wisdom
Which was able to delve
Down to how things
Really are,

And mounted it upon
The steed of quietude,
Which remains unmoved.

So they took up the razor sword
Of the reasoning of
The middle way,
Free of extremes—

Which allowed them to destroy
All of them, for their habit

Of holding to things
In an extreme way.

[260]

(37)
,TSUL BZHIN DPYOD PA'I YANGS PA'I SHES RAB KYIS,
,DE NYID RTOGS PA'I BLO GROS RGYAS PAR MDZAD,
,RNAL 'BYOR NGAS KYANG NYAMS LEN DE LTAR BGYIS,
,THAR 'DOD KHYED KYANG DE BZHIN BSKYANG 'TSAL LO,

They found a vast form of wisdom
That performed its analysis
With total accuracy,

And were able to expand
That high intelligence which
Allowed them to realize suchness.

I, the deep practitioner,
Have accomplished my practice
This way;

And you who hope for freedom
Should do your practice
The same.

[261]
DMIGS PA LA **RTZE GCIG** PA'I **BSAM GTAN TZAM LA 'KHOR
BA YI RTZA BA** MA RIG PA RTZAD NAS **GCOD PA'I NUS PA MA
MTHONG ZHING,**

We can't see that single-pointed meditation on a particular
object of focus *would possess, by itself, sufficient power
to sever the root of the cycle of pain*—our tendency to
misunderstand things—at its very core.

[262]
DE LTA [f. 9b] NA'ANG DMIGS PA LA RTZE GCIG TU GNAS PA'I **ZHI
GNAS** KYI **LAM DANG BRAL BA'I** THOS BSAM GYI **SHES RAB KYIS**
KYANG,

Even so, we can say something similar with that form of wisdom which derives from learning & contemplation alone: *wisdom which is divorced from the path of quietude,* which itself remains focused single-pointedly upon its intended object.

[263]
BDEN MED SOGS KYI DPYAD DON LA **JI TZAM DPYAD KYANG NYON MONGS** RTZAD NAS **MI LDOG PAS** NA,

That is, with this alone *we can perform as much examination as we want* towards objects of analysis such as the fact that nothing is real; *but still we will find ourselves unable to put a stop to our negative emotions* by tearing them out from the root.

[264]
SNGON GYI DAM PAS DE KHO NA NYID KYI DON TSUL BZHIN DU GO BA'I **YIN LUGS** KYI DON LA **PHU THAG CHOD PA'I SHES RAB DE,**

Here then is what holy ones of the past did. First *they took* their wisdom—*a form of wisdom which was able to delve,* perfectly, *down to* the point of *how things really are:* a wisdom with which they comprehended, accurately, the meaning of suchness.

[265]
DE KHO NA NYID LA BYING RGOD KYI RNAM RTOG GIS **G-YO** BA MED PA'I **ZHI GNAS** KYI **RTA LA BSKYON NAS NI,**

And then they *mounted* this wisdom *upon the steed of quietude, which remains unmoved* by dullness & agitation, in its focus upon suchness.

[266]
RTAG CHAD KYI **MTHA'** DANG **BRAL** BA'I **DBU MA'I RIGS PA**
GCIG DU BRAL LA SOGS PA'**I MTSON RNON GYIS** NI,

And *so they took up the razor sword of the reasoning of the
middle way, free of* the *extremes* of things either never
changing, or else simply discontinuing. That is, they
employed logic such as the proof of neither one nor
many.[46]

[267]
RTAG PA DANG CHAD PA'I MTHAR 'DZIN PA'**I MTHAR 'DZIN** GYI
DMIGS PA'I **GTAD** SO BDEN GRUB TU BZUNG BA LTAR

Which is to say, we all have a tendency to hold things
as existing in a real sense: a *habit of holding to things in an
extreme way,* which means that at bottom we think that
things could either never change, or simply disappear.

[268]
BDEN 'DZIN GYI ZHEN YUL **THAMS CAD 'JIG** PAR **BYED PA'I** RIGS
PA YANG DAG PA'I DON LA **TSUL BZHIN DU DPYOD PA'I YANGS
PA'I SHES RAB KYIS**

But these wise ones utilized a form of clear thinking
which *allowed them to destroy all* the objects that their habit
of seeing things as real thought it was observing: *they
found a vast form of wisdom that performed its analysis with*

---

[46] *Proof of neither one nor many:* One of nearly countless classical proofs of
emptiness; the classical form of the syllogism goes like this:
    Consider the knowledge of the basis, the knowledge of
        the path, and omniscience itself [three levels of
        emptiness understanding];
    None of them exists in truth,
    Because they are devoid of both existing truly as a single thing,
        and existing truly as more than one thing.
    They are, for example, like a reflection in a mirror.
See for example f. 45b of the *Jewel Lamp* of Jamyang Shepay Dorje,
Ngawang Tsundru (1648-1721) (B5, S19088).

total accuracy, regarding the real nature of things.

[269]
DE KHO NA NYID RTOGS PA'I BLO GROS RGYAS PAR MDZAD DO,,

That is, they *were able to expand that high intelligence which allowed them to realize suchness.*

Instructions for quietude + insight

[270]
GNYIS PA NI, RTZE GCIG GOMS PAS SOGS DRUG STE,

Which brings us to our second part here: the actual instructions for this particular type of meditation. We find this in the six lines[47] of the root text [in the Tibetan] which include "accustoming ourselves to remaining single-pointed":

[271]

(38)
,RTZE GCIG GOMS PAS TING 'DZIN 'GRUB PA NI,
,SMOS PAR CI 'TSAL TSUL BZHIN DPYOD PA YI,
,SO SOR RTOG PA YIS KYANG YIN LUGS LA,
,G-YO MED SHIN TU BRTAN PAR GNAS PA YI,

**What need to mention
Accustoming ourselves
To remaining single-pointed,
And reaching
One-point concentration?**

---

[47] *Six lines:* Again, not counting the refrain.

We then move into
Specific individual understandings,
Through accurate analysis.

Through this, we see
That we can give birth
To a fixed concentration

That can remain,
Very solidly
And without shifting,
On the way things
Really are.

[272]

(39)

,TING 'DZIN BSKYED PAR MTHONG NAS ZHE {%ZHI} LHAG
GNYIS,
,ZUNG 'BREL SGRUB LA BRTZON RNAMS YA MTSAN NO,
,RNAL 'BYOR NGAS KYANG NYAMS LEN DE LTAR BGYIS,
,THAR 'DOD KHYED KYANG DE BZHIN BSKYANG 'TSAL LO,

Those who make intense efforts
Towards achieving the two
Of quietude & special insight

In combination
Are truly wondrous.

I, the deep practitioner,
Have accomplished my practice
This way;

And you who hope for freedom
Should do your practice
The same.

[273]
RANG GI DMIGS PA GANG RUNG CIG LA DMIGS NAS MI DPYOD
PAR **RTZE GCIG** TU GNAS PA **GOMS PAS TING** NGE 'DZIN 'GRUB
PAR 'GYUR BA **NI** GZHIR BCAS SHING

And so let us consider that state of wisdom where we
have *accustomed ourselves to remaining single-pointed* upon
any one particular object of focus, without engaging in
some particular analysis—that is, where we have *reached
one-point concentration*, and taken this as our starting
point.

[274]
SMOS PA CI 'TSAL TE BRJOD MI DGOS KYI,

And *what need* really do we have *to mention* this focus
here? We can assume it.

[275]
DMIGS PA LA RTZE GCIG TU GNAS BZHIN PA'I NGANG NAS DON
LA **TSUL BZHIN** DU **DPYOD PA YI SO SOR RTOGS PA YI** SHES RAB
KYIS **KYANG**

Keeping in this state where we maintain a single point
of focus on the particular object involved, *we then move
into* that wisdom where we can have *specific individual
understandings,*[48] *through* an *accurate analysis* of the object.

[276]
YIN LUGS KYI DON **LA G-YO** BA **MED** PAR **SHIN TU BRTAN PAR**

---

[48] *Individual understandings:* It appears that the standard Tibetan spelling
of the term that we have translated as "individual understandings" here
is *so-sor rtog-pa;* the English translation is supported by the most common
Sanskrit original, which is *pratyavekṣa.* And this is how we find the
spelling in our root text. But we also frequently see Tibetan writers using
so-sor rtogs-pa, as we do here in the commentary, which would tend more
to mean "individual realizations," or a more direct sort of perception. It
seems that what is meant here is more the understanding.

GNAS PA YI TING 'DZIN SKYED PAR NUS PA BLOS **MTHONG NAS**

It all starts when, *through this,* our mind *"sees"* that we have the power to *give birth to a fixed concentration that can remain, very solidly and without shifting, on* the particular object of *the way things really are.*

[277]
ZHI LHAG GNYIS LAS PHYOGS RE TZAM MA YIN PAR **ZUNG 'BREL SGRUB** PAR BYED PA **LA BRTZON** PA **RNAMS YA MTSAN NO** STE NGO MTSAR CHE'O,,

And so *those who make intense efforts towards achieving the two of quietude & special insight in combination*—without just one side or the other—*are truly wondrous,* truly amazing.

[278]
RANG GI DMIGS PA LA GTOD DE RTZE GCIG TU GNAS PA GOMS KYANG ZHI GNAS 'GRUB MOD

Now it is admittedly the case that—if we become accustomed to directing our mind towards its particular object, and remaining there single-pointedly—we can achieve quietude.

[279]
LHAG MTHONG 'GRUB PA LA NI, DE TZAM GYIS MCHOG {%MA CHOG} PAR RTZE GCIG TU GNAS BZHIN PA'I DAD {%NGANG} NAS DPYAD STOBS KYIS SHIN SBYANGS KYI BDE BA 'DREN NUS PA DANG DGOS PA'I DON NO,,

But this alone is not enough, if we hope to go on to attain special insight. The point here then is that we have to be able to—and in fact we *must*—reach a state of single-pointed focus, and then staying in that focus use our powers of examination to bring on the bliss of physical & mental litheness.

Conducting a session
in two periods

[280]

GSUM PA NI, MNYAM GZHAG NAM MKHA' SOGS DRUG STE,

This brings us to our third section from before: how to conduct both periods of a session—both balanced meditation and the aftermath period, along with some ancillary points. This point is expressed in the six lines [in the Tibetan] which include "balanced meditation... like empty space":

[281]

(40)

,MNYAM GZHAG NAM MKHA' LTA BU'I STONG NYID DANG,
,RJES THOB SGYU MA LTA BU'I STONG PA GNYIS,
,BSGOMS NAS THABS SHES ZUNG DU 'BREL BA YIS,
,RGYAL SRAS SPYOD PA'I PHA ROL 'GRO BAR BSNGAGS,

We continue to meditate
Upon these two:

Emptiness which is like
Empty space,
In a balanced meditation;

And then emptiness
In this aftermath,
Where things are
Like an illusion.

This is highly praised
As a journey to the far side
Of the activities

Of the children
Of the Victors;

Through a combination

Of the two
Of method & wisdom.

[282]

(41)

,DE LTAR RTOGS NAS PHYOGS RE'I LAM GYIS NI,
,TSIM PA MED PA SKAL BZANG RNAMS KYI LUGS,
,RNAL 'BYOR NGAS KYANG NYAMS LEN DE LTAR BGYIS,
,THAR 'DOD KHYED KYANG DE BZHIN BSKYANG 'TSAL LO,

Having come to this realization,
It is the way of those
Who have within them
Rich power of good deeds

To never be satisfied
With a path consisting of
Only either one of the pair.
I, the deep practitioner,
Have accomplished my practice
This way;

And you who hope for freedom
Should do your practice
The same.

[283]
DE KHO NA NYID KYI DON LA MNYAM PAR BZHAG PA'I **MNYAM GZHAG** DGAG BYA BDEN GRUB BKAG PA'I **NAM MKHA' LTA BU'I STONG NYID** SGOM PA **DANG**,

Now first here we are meditating upon an *emptiness which is like empty space:* this is a *balanced meditation* where we are sitting in balance on the object of suchness, and where we have succeeded in putting a stop to that thing which the concept of emptiness denies; that is, a state where things could exist in truth.

[284]
DE LAS YANGS {%LANGS} NAS **RJES THOB** TU BDEN PAR SNANG
[f. 10a] YANG DER MA GRUB PA'I **SGYU MA LTA BU'I STONG PA**
NYID

And then at some point we come out of this meditation;
and *in this aftermath,* things still appear to us as though
they existed in truth. But we know that they do not, and
so here is a second kind of *emptiness where things are like
an illusion.*

[285]
GNYIS PO **BSGOMS NAS**, SBYIN PA LA SOGS PA **THABS** DANG,
STONG NYID RTOGS PA'I **SHES** RAB GNYIS KA **ZUNG DU 'BREL
BA YI** SGO NAS

And so *we continue to meditate upon these two* kinds of
emptiness; and then we are able to achieve a *combination
of the two: of* both *"method,"* which refers to the perfections
of giving and the like; and *"wisdom,"* where we enjoy a
realization of emptiness.

[286]
RGYAL SRAS SPYOD PA RGYA MTSO'I **PHA ROL** TU **'GRO BA** NI
RGYAL DANG DE SRAS RNAMS KYIS **BSNGAGS** SO,,

With this, we are able to make a successful *journey to the
far side of* the ocean of *the activities of the children of the
Victors;* this then is the way that is so *highly praised* by
these very Victors, and their offspring.

[287]
RJES THOB TU SGYU MA LTA BU BSGOMS PA NI STONG NYID
SGOM PA DNGOS MIN NA'ANG PHYOGS MTHUN YIN PAS DENG
{%DER} BTAGS PA TZAM MO,,

Now we should note though here that meditating—
during the aftermath of the direct perception of
emptiness—on how things are like an illusion is not,

technically, itself the direct perception of emptiness. But since it is so closely aligned with that perception, we are just referring to it as if it were.

[288]
JI SKAD BSHAD PA **DE LTAR RTOGS NAS** THABS SHES **PHYOGS RE** BA'I **LAM GYIS NI TSIM PA MED PA SKAL BZANG RNAMS KYI LUGS** SO,,

And so *it is the way of those who have within them rich power of good deeds to never be satisfied with a path consisting of only either one of the pair*—of method and wisdom. For they have *come to a realization* of the points we have here described.

The way of the secret word

[289]
GNYIS PA THUN THOR {%THUN MONG} MA YIN PA SNGAGS KYI THEG PA LA BSLA {%BSLAB} TSUL NI, DE LTAR RGYU DANG 'BRAS BU'I THEG CHEN GYI, ,SOGS DRUG STE,

With this, we have reached our second major division from before: an explanation of how we practice the path of the unique steps: the way of the secret word. This point is conveyed in the six lines which include "supreme paths within the greater way: that of the causes, and also of the results":

[290]
(42)
,DE LTAR RGYU DANG 'BRAS BU'I THEG CHEN GYI,
,LAM MCHOG GNYIS KAR DGOS PA'I THUN MONG LAM,
,JI BZHIN BSKYED NAS MKHAS PA'I DED DPON GYI,
,MGON LA BRTEN NAS RGYUD SDE'I RGYA MTSO CHER,

That kind is a pathway

That is shared:
One which is necessary
For both of these
Supreme paths
Within the greater way:

That of the causes,
And also of the results.

We give birth to it
In exactly the right way;

And with that,
We must take ourselves
To someone who becomes
Our savior:
A ship captain
Who is a master.

We set off with them
Across the vast sea
Of the secret teachings.

[291]

(43)

,ZHUGS NAS YONGS RDZOGS MAN NGAG BSTEN PA DES,
,DAL 'BYOR THOB PA DON DANG LDAN PAR BYAS,
,RNAL 'BYOR NGAS KYANG NYAMS LEN DE LTAR BGYIS,
,THAR 'DOD KHYOD KYANG DE BZHIN BSKYANG 'TSAL LO,

We become
One of those people
Who is able to
Surrender themselves

To these private advices,
Which contain
The absolute entirety.

With this,
We have truly
Given some meaning

To the fact that
We came into this life
With all the different
Leisures & fortunes.

I, the deep practitioner,
Have accomplished my practice
This way;

And you who hope for freedom
Should do your practice
The same.

[292]
SNGAR BSHAD PA **DE LTAR** LAM BGROD TSUL DE NI, **RGYU** PHA ROL TU PHYIN PA'I THEG PA **DANG**,

Now let's consider *that kind* of method of travelling the path which we have explained in the lines up to here. This is what we refer to as the "way of *causes*" — referring to the various perfections.

[293]
'BRAS BU SNGAGS KYI THEG PA'**I THEG CHEN GYI LAM MCHOG GNYIS** GAR {%KAR} **DGOS PA'I THUN MONG** BA'I **LAM** YIN LA, DE **JI** LTA BA **BZHIN** RGYUD LA **BSKYED** DE,

But there is *also* the "way of the *results*," a reference to the way of the secret word. And what we have been describing here is a *pathway which is shared: one which is necessary for both of these supreme paths within the greater way.* What *we* seek to do is to *give birth* to this shared

140

pathway, and to do that *in exactly the right way.*

[294]
DE **NAS** SNAGS {%SNGAGS} LA **MKHAS PA'I DED DPON GYI MGON** RDO RJE SLOB DPON **LA BRTEN NAS RGYUD SDE'I RGYA** MSO {%**MTSO**} CHEN POR ZHUGS NAS

With that, we must take ourselves to someone who becomes our savior: a ship captain who is a master in the
way of the secret word. *With* her, or him, *we set off across the vast sea of* these *secret teachings.*

[295]
MDO SNGAGS GNYIS KYI LAM GYI GNAD **YONGS** SU **RDZOGS** PA'I **MAN NGAG BSTEN PA'I** GANG ZAG **DES, DAL 'BYOR** GYI LUS RTEN 'DI **THOB PA DON DANG LDAN PAR BYAS** PA YIN NO,,

Suppose thus that *we become one of those people who is able to surrender themselves to these private advices, which contain* in their *absolute entirety* all the crucial points of the path of both the open & secret ways. *With this, we have truly given some meaning to the fact that we came into this life with* a body & mind complete in *all the different leisures & fortunes.*

[296]
RJE BTZUN SOGS SNGAR LTAR RO,,

The lines then about the "holy Lamas" are to be understood as they have been, up to here.

The conclusion

[297]
GSUM PA MJUG NI, RANG GI YID LA SOGS DRUG STE,

This brings us to our third and final portion of the entire composition: the details of its closing section. This is expressed in the six lines [of the Tibetan] which include "in order to accustom my mind":

[298]

(44)

,RANG GI YID LA GOMS PAR BYA PHYIR DANG,
,SKAL BZANG GZHAN LA'ANG PHAN PAR BYA BA'I PHYIR,
,RGYAL BA DGYES PA'I YONGS SU RDZOGS PA'I LAM,
,GO SLA'I NGAG GIS BSHAD PA'I DGE BA DES,

In order to accustom
My mind to it,

And also to provide
My help to others
Who truly possess

Enough good karma,
Within them,

I have presented
This explanation

Of the complete entirety
Of the path which has pleased
The Victors themselves,

In wording
Quite easy to comprehend.

[299]

(45)

,'GRO BA KUN KYANG RNAM DAG LAM BZANG DANG,
,'BRAL MED GYUR CIG CES NA {%NI} SMON LAM 'DEBS,
,RNAL 'BYOR NGAS KYANG [f. 58a] SMON LAM DE LTAR BTAB,
,THAR 'DOD KHYED KYANG DE BZHIN 'DEBS 'TSAL LO,

And I make a solemn prayer that,
By this good karma
Which I have collected,

Each & every
Living being there is

May never be separated
From this pure
And beautiful path.

I, the deep practitioner,
Have made my prayers this way;

And you who hope for freedom
Should make your prayers the same.

[300]
RANG GI YID LA GOMS PAR BYA BA'I **PHYIR DANG**, DON GNYER CAN GYI **SKAL BZANG GZHAN LA'ANG PHAN PAR BYA BA'I PHYIR** DU,

I have undertaken this composition *in order to accustom my mind to its* contents; *and also to provide my help to others* who might aspire to these practices: to those *who truly possess enough good karma, within them.*

[301]
RGYAL BA DGYES PA'I YONGS SU RDZOGS PA'I LAM MDOR BSDUS NAS, **GO SLA'I NGAG GIS**

For this then, I have created a brief summary of *the complete entirety of the path which has pleased the Victors themselves.* To do so, I have done my best to use *wording* which would be *quite easy to comprehend.*

[302]
BSHAD PA'I DGE BA DES NI, PHYOGS RE TZAM MA YIN PAR **'GRO BA KUN KYANG RNAM DAG LAM BZANG** 'DI DANG, **'BRAL** BA MED PAR **GYUR CIG CES NI SMON LAM 'DEBS** SO,,

And I would here like to dedicate *the good karma which I have collected through presenting this explanation.* That is, *I here make a solemn prayer that, by this, each & every living being there is*—and not just some part of them—*may never be separated from this pure and beautiful path.*

[303]
RJE BTZUN BLA MAS SOGS SAM, **RNAL 'BYOR NGAS KYANG SMON LAM** [f. 10b] **DE LTAR BTAB, ,THAR 'DOD KHYED KYANG DE BZHIN 'DEBS 'TSAL LO,** ,ZHES PA GANG BYAS KYANG DON NI SLA'O,,

In closing here there are two options. First, we could read the lines as we find them here—

> *I, the deep practitioner,*
> *Have made my prayers this way;*

> *And you who hope for freedom*
> *Should make your prayers the same.*

Or else you could read the lines using "the holy Lamas." Either way, the meaning is easily understood.

[304]
'DI'I 'PHROR STON PA BLA NA MED PA'I BSTAN PA DANG, ,ZHES SOGS TSIGS BCAD GCIG DANG,

Now there is a general custom that three different prayers are added here at the end. One of them reads:

[305]
[,STON PA BLA NA MED PA'I BSTAN PA DANG,
,MJAL BA 'DI 'DRA BLA MA'I DRIN YIN PAS,
,DGE BA 'DI YANG 'GRO BA MA LUS PA,

,BSHES GNYEN DAM PAS 'DZIN PA'I RGYU RU BSNGO,]

> The fact that I have met this way
> With the teaching of
> The Teacher Beyond All Teachers
>
> Is due to the great kindness
> Of my own Lama.
>
> And so I dedicate
> All the good karma
> Of the deed I've accomplished here
>
> That every single living being
> Might come into the care
> Of a holy spiritual friend
> Of their own.[49]

[306]
NGA YI BLA MA BLO BZANG GRAGS PA DE, ,ZHES SOGS TSIGS
BCAD GCIG DANG,

The second prayer goes like this:

[307]
[,NGA YI BLA MA BLO BZANG GRAGS PA DE,
,DGA' LDAN GNAS SAM BDE BA CAN LA SOGS,
,DAG PA'I ZHING KHAMS GANG NA BZHUGS KYANG RUNG,
,BDAG SOGS 'KHOR GYI THOG MAR SKYE PAR {%BAR} SHOG]

> Now my Lama, Lobsang Drakpa,
> May be sitting right now

---

[49] *Come into the care:* Our commentator has mentioned only the opening line of each of the three verses mentioned, since they would be quite familiar to any monastic reading his work. For our reader's benefit, we have inserted the full prayer in each case. This first one is found in Je Tsongkapa's famous praise of the Buddha for teaching dependence from the point of view of emptiness (f. 15b, B9, S05275-15).

In the Paradise of Bliss,
Or the Heaven of Happiness;

Or in some other one
Of the realms of total purity.
But wherever he may be,
I make this prayer

That I and those with me
Might be reborn

In the front row
Of the disciples
Gathered around him now.[50]

[308]
DANG POR RGYA CHEN THOS PA MANG DU BTZAL, ,ZHES SOGS
TSIGS BCAD GCIG STE TSIGS BCAD GSUM 'BYUNG BA NI,

And the third prayer reads:

[309]
[,DANG POR RGYA CHEN THOS PA MANG DU BTZAL,
,BAR DU GZHUNG LUGS THAMS CAD GDAMS PAR SHAR,
,THA MAR NYIN MTSAN KUN TU NYAMS SU BLANGS,
,KUN KYANG BSTAN PA RGYAS PA'I CHED DU BSNGOS,]

The first thing
You need to do
Is to seek vast learning.

---

[50] *Reborn in the front row:* We have excerpted this verse from a commentary
to the famous "Thousand Angels of the Heaven of Bliss," an oral tradition
granted by Je Tsongkapa himself and first put into writing by Gyuchen
Sangye Gyatso (born c. 1550), a teacher of His Holiness the First Panchen
Lama, Lobsang Chukyi Gyeltsen (1565-1662). See f. 6a of *A Dissection
Presentation Related to the Lama Practice Called "The Thousand Angels of the
Heaven of Bliss," along with Private Instructions* (B7, S19001).

Next, make all
The classics dawn
In your mind as personal advice.
And then finally,
Work day & night
To put these things into practice—
And remember to dedicate
All of it, so that
The teachings should spread in this world.[51]

[310]
GZHAN GYIS 'DON CHA LA KHA BKANG BA STE, 'DI'I MJUG
DNGOS MIN PAS MA BRIS SO,,

The custom of reciting these three after *The Song* though
represents a later addition; as such, they are not a part of
the original conclusion, and I shall not cover them here.

The colophon

[311]
(colophon)
,ZHES BYANG CHUB LAM GYI RIM PA'I NYAMS LEN
GYI RNAM GZHAG MDOR BSDUS TE BRJED BYANG
DU BYAS PA 'DI NI, MANG DU THOS PA'I DGE SLONG
SPONG BA PA BLO BZANG GRAGS PA'I DPAL GYIS,
,'BROG RI BO CHE DGE LDAN RNAM PAR RGYAL BA'I
GLING DU SBYAR BA'O,, ,,

**This then is a brief presentation on how
to put into practice the various steps of the
path to enlightenment, written out to help
me remember all the points. It has been**

---

[51] The teachings should spread in this world: We've excerpted the full
verse from f. 8a of Notes to a Teaching on the "Thousand Angels of the
Heaven of Bliss," a Lama Practice, written by Gungtang Konchok Tenpay
Drunme (1762-1823) (B1, S00930).

composed by a very learned monk who has given up the world: by the glorious [Je Tsongkapa,] Lobsang Drakpa. The work was completed at the monastery known as Ganden, land of goodness, isle of the final victory, nestled below Shepherd's Peak.

[312]
ZHES BYANG CHUB LAM GYI RIM PA'I NYAMS LEN GYI RNAM GZHAG MDOR BSDUS TE BRJED BYANG DU BYAS PA 'DI NI, MANG DU THOS PA'I DGE SLONG SPONG BA PA BLO BZANG GRAGS PA'I DPAL GYIS 'BROG RI BO CHE DGE LDAN RNAM PAR RGYAL BA'I GLING DU SBYAR BA'O, ,ZHES PA NI SLA'O,,

The final words of the text here are easily understood:

This then is a brief presentation on how to put into practice the various steps of the path to enlightenment, written out to help me remember all the points. It has been composed by a very learned monk who has given up the world: by the glorious [Je Tsongkapa,] Lobsang Drakpa. The work was completed at the monastery known as Ganden, land of goodness, isle of the final victory, nestled below Shepherd's Peak.

[313]
'DIR BYANG CHUB LAM GYI RIM PA'I GNAD TSANG BAS, 'DON PA'I TSE DAL BUS DON YID LA BSHAD {%SHAR} PAR BYAS NA LAM RIM GYI DON BSDUS NAS NYAMS SU BLANGS PAR 'GYUR YANG, TSIG TZAM TON PAS NI MIN NO,,

Now all the crucial points of the steps of the path to enlightenment may be found here in this work, complete. As such, when you recite the text out loud, you should do so in a relaxed way, pausing to allow yourself to reflect upon each separate point. If you do it like this, then you are actually carrying out a brief practice of the entire series of the steps to the path. This is not the case though if you just sit and recite the words.

[314]
DES NA 'DI KHA TON BYED PAS NI, DBYANGS KYI SGRA SNYAN PA TZAM LA CHAGS PAR MI BYA'O,,

As such, we can say that whenever you chant a work like this, you should try not to just get wrapped up in how beautiful the recitation sounds to you.

[315]
'DIR NYAMS SU LEN TSUL RGYAS PAR LAM RIM DANG SBYAR NAS 'CHAD NUS NA'ANG MANG DU DOGS SHING,

Now I could have made my explanation of these lines here by connecting each topic over to one of the major classics on the steps of the path, and created a practice manual that was much more detailed. But I was afraid that then the work would become too long.

[316]
DMIGS SKOR ZHIG LOGS SU BRIS YOD PAS RGYAS PAR MA BSHAD LA, TSIG DON RDZOGS PAR SNGAR GZHAN GYIS BKRAL BA MA MTHONG YANG RANG BLOS CI NUS KYIS BKRAL BA'O,,

Moreover, I have described each of the various practice topics here in detail, elsewhere; and so have not done so here. But in fact I have never seen a commentary by anyone else that presented the meaning of the entire wording of the original lines; and so I have done so here, to the very best of my ability.

Closing verses

[317]
,,SMRAS PA,

149

And so it is done.

[318]

,RGYAL BA'I GSUNG RAB KUN GYI SNYING PO'I DON,
,NYAMS SU LEN PA'I DOM {%RIM} PAR RAB BSGRIL BA,
,BYANG CHUB BGROD PA'I LAM GYI RIM PA 'DI,
,THUB BSTAN RGYAL MTSAN RTZE NA NOR BU BZHIN,

It encapsulates the essential meaning
Of all the high speech of the Victors;
Setting out all the stages of practice.

This presentation of the steps
Of the path to enlightenment
Is a jewel mounted atop the flagpole
Of the banner of victory for
The teachings of the Able One.

[319]

,DE PHYIR TSUL 'DIR NYAMS LEN PHYOGS TZAM ZHIG
,BGYIS PA YIS KYANG SKAL BAR LDAN 'GYUR NA,
,JI SKAD BSHAD BZHIN RDZOGS PAR NYAMS LEN DU,
,BSTAR [f. 11a] BA GANG YIN NGO MTSAR CIS MI CHE,

As such, you will become
A person of great blessedness

Even if all that you ever do
Is to put into personal practice
Just some portion of this way.

Why then wouldn't it be
Completely amazing if one
Were actually able to carry out
Everything we've described here?

[320]

,GZHUNG DON CHA SHAS YONGS RDZOGS KUN DA'I
GNYEN,
,THUB BSTAN LHA LAM MDZES PAR BYA PHYIR DANG,

,'GRO 'DI'I KHAMS KYI SGRIB MUN BSAL BA'I CHED,
,LHAG BSAM DAG PA'I MGYOGS 'GRO'I {=rta} SHUGS
KYIS DRANGS,

This friend of the jasmine,
Which incorporates every single
Component of the meaning
Of the classical scriptures,

Has been drawn forth
By the racers of complete
Personal responsibility—

So that the road of the gods,
The teachings of the Able Ones,
Might be made even more
Stunningly beautiful;

And the darkness in the realms
Within these living beings,

Obscuring their hearts,
Might forever be cleared away.[52]

[321]

,'DIR 'BAD 'O MTSO LAS 'KHRUNGS RNAM DKAR GYI,
,DGE LEGS BDUD RTZIS DON GNYER LDAN PA YI,
,'CHI MED YID KYI RE BA YONGS RDZOGS TE,
,GTAN BDE SROG GI NYER 'TSOR 'GYUR BAR SHOG

And so here is
An alabaster nectar
Of virtue & goodness

---

[52] *Forever cleared away:* As is traditional, the verse is filled with classical poeticisms that date back to ancient India. The friend of the night-blooming jasmine is the moon, whose rays coax its petals open. Moon & sun are both seen as moving across the sky mounted on a grand chariot drawn by massive mythical horses, called "racers." The "road of the gods" is a reference to the sky.

Distilled from the depths
Of the ocean of milk—

May it fulfil all the hopes
Of deathlessness for all
Who might aspire to it;

May it serve as sustenance
For sustaining the life
Of their everlasting joy.[53]

[322]
,CES BYANG CHUB LAM GYI RIM PA'I BSDUS DON GYI TSIG 'PHREL
{%'GREL} SNYING PO MDOR BSDUS GSAL BA ZHES BYA BA 'DI NI,

This then concludes *A Brief Clarification of the Heart: A Word-by-Word Commentary to "An Abbreviated Presentation of the Steps to the Path to Enlightenment."*

[323]
DAD DANG RNAM DPYOD ZUNG DU 'BREL BA'I KHYA'O LUNG
DGA' {%BKA'} BCU PA BLO BZANG BSAM 'GRUB KYIS BSKUL BA'I
NGOR,

It was composed at the urgent behest of that Master of the Ten Classics, Lobsang Samdrup of the Land of Kyao, who combines within him both great faith and intellectual acumen.

[324]
SH'AKYA'I DGE SLONG BSHAD SGRUB MING CAN GYIS 'PHRAL
DU MGYOGS LAS SU BRIS PA STE, PHYIS BAR {%PAR} DU BRKO BA'I
TSE YI GE BA'ANG BSKUL BA PO NYID DO,,

---

[53] *Sustain the life of everlasting joy:* This entire verse is a reference to an ancient Indian myth known as *Samudra Manthana:* the churning of an ocean of milk by the gods—using the central mountain of the world as a churning stick—to produce the nectar of immortality.

The text was written by myself—a Buddhist monk who holds the name of "Shedrup"—working as fast as I could, with only little time to do so. Later, when it came time to carve the piece onto blocks, the scribal work was performed by that same monk who made the original request.

[325]
'DIS KYANG RGYAL BA'I BSTAN PA RIN PO CHE PHYOGS THAMS CAD DU DAR ZHING RGYAS LA YUN RING DU GNAS PAR GYUR CIG,

And I pray that—through the efforts I've made here— the precious teaching of the Victorious Buddhas might spread & flourish throughout many lands, and remain there for a very long time to come.

[326]
,,DGE'O,,

It is good.

The root text of Je Tsongkapa's
Song of My Spiritual Life

(1)
`,,PHUN TSOGS DGE LEGS BYE BAS BSKRUN PA'I SKU,
,MTHA' YAS 'GRO BA'I RE BA SKONG BA'I GSUNG,
,MA LUS SHES BYA JI BZHIN GZIGS PA'I THUGS,
,SH'AKYA'I GTZO BO DE LA MGOS PHYAG 'TSAL,

> Your holy body
> Was birthed by
> Billions of perfect
> Good deeds;
>
> Your holy words
> Fulfil the hopes
> Of infinite living beings;
>
> Your holy mind
> Sees all things
> In the universe
> Exactly as they are;
>
> I touch my head
> To the feet
> Of that leader
> Of the Shakya clan.

(2)
,ZLA MED STON PA DE YI SRAS KYI MCHOG
,RGYAL BA'I MDZAD PA KUN GYI KHUR BSNAMS NAS,
,GRANGS MED ZHING DU SPRUL PAS RNAM ROL BA,

,MI PHAM 'JAM PA'I DBYANGS LA PHYAG 'TSAL LO,

> I bow down to
> The Undefeatable,
> And to Gentle Voice:
>
> The two highest children
> Of the matchless Teacher,
>
> Who took upon themselves
> The heavy load
> Of all the Victor's deeds,
>
> Engaging in the divine play
> With emanations sent
> To countless different realms.

(3)
,SHIN TU DPAG PAR DKA' BA RGYAL BA'I YUM,
,JI BZHIN DGONGS PA 'GREL MDZAD 'DZAM GLING RGYAN,
,KLU SGRUB THOGS MED CES NI SA GSUM NA,
,YONGS SU GRAGS PA'I ZHABS LA BDAG PHYAG 'TSAL,

> I prostrate
> At the holy feet
> Of those known
> As Nagarjuna & Asanga,
>
> So widely famed
> Through the three realms.
>
> You are true jewels
> Of our world
> Who undertook
> To comment,
>
> In a perfectly
> Accurate way,

Upon the true thought
Of the Mother Sutras
Of the Victors,

So extremely difficult
To fathom.

(4)
,SHING RTA CHEN PO GNYIS LAS LEGS BRGYUD PA'I,
,ZAB MO'I LTA BA RGYA CHEN SPYOD PA'I LAM,
,MA NOR YONGS SU RDZOGS PA'I GNAD BSDUS PA'I,
,GDAMS PA'I MDZOD 'DZIN MAR ME MDZAD LA 'DUD,

I bow down to
Dipankara,
Maker of Lamps,

Who holds a great treasure
Of advices which incorporate,
Unerringly,

Each & every one of
The essential points

Of the paths
Of the profound view
And widespread activities

Descended so perfectly
From the two
Great innovators.

(5)
,RAB 'BYAMS GSUNG RAB KUN LA LTA BA'I MIG
,SKAL BZANG THAR PAR BGROD PA'I 'JUG NGOGS MCHOG
,BRTZE BAS BSKYOD PA'I THABS MKHAS MDZAD PA YIS,
,GSAL MDZAD BSHES GNYEN RNAMS LA GUS PHYAG 'TSAL,

I bow down
To all those spiritual friends
Who utilize a variety
Of skillful means

To clarify these teachings,
Moved by their love.

They are eyes to view
All of the myriad forms
Of high teachings—

 The very highest
Point of entry for those
Of sufficient goodness

To make the journey
To freedom.

(6)
,'DZAM GLING MKHAS PA YONGS KYI GTZUG GI RGYAN,
,SNYAN PA'I BA DAN 'GRO NA LHANG NGE BA,
,KLU SGRUB THOGS MED GNYIS LAS RIM BZHIN DU,
,LEGS BRGYUD BYANG CHUB LAM GYI RIM PA NI,

The steps on the path
To enlightenment,

Passed down
With such excellence,
In their own stages,
Through the two
Of Nagarjuna and Asanga,

Are a jewel on the topknot
Of each & every master
Upon this planet;

A victory banner
Of great renown,
Glorious here
Among beings.

(7)
,SKYE DGU'I 'DOD DON MA LUS SKONG BAS NA,
,GDAMS PA RIN CHEN DBANG GI RGYAL PO STE,
,GZHUNG BZANG STONG GI CHU BO 'DU BA'I PHYIR,
,DPAL LDAN LEGS PAR BSHAD PA'I RGYA MTSO'ANG YIN,

These are an instruction
Which is the very king
Among the lords
Of all jewels,

For they fulfil
Each & every one of the
Aspirations of beings.

They combine the rivers
Of a thousand
Beautiful classics;

As such, they are
A glorious ocean
Of fine explanation.

(8)
,BSTAN PA THAMS CAD 'GAL MED RTOGS PA DANG,
,GSUNG RAB MA LUS GDAMS PAR 'CHAR BA DANG,
,RGYAL BA'I DGONGS PA BDE BLAG RNYED [f. 56a] PA DANG,
,NYES SPYOD CHEN PO'I G-YANG SA LAS KYANG BSRUNG,

The steps also allow us
To grasp that each one
Of the teachings

Is completely compatible
With all the others.

They also make it possible
For all the classic teachings
Of the Buddha to strike us

As advice meant for
Each of us, personally.

They permit us to locate,
With perfect ease,
The true intent of the Victors.

And we are also
Protected from
Falling off the high cliff
Of the Great Mistake.

(9)
,DE PHYIR RGYA BOD MKHAS PA'I SKYE BO NI,
,SKAL LDAN DU MAS BSTEN PA'I GDAMS PA MCHOG
,SKYES BU GSUM GYI LAM GYI RIM PA YIS,
,YID RAB MI 'PHROG DPYOD LDAN SU ZHIG YOD,

As such, the steps
Are a supreme form
Of instruction

Relied upon
By a great many people
Of sufficient goodness—
By great masters—
In both India and Tibet.

Where could we find
A person with intelligence

Whose heart wasn't
Completely stolen away

By these steps of the path
Designed for persons
Of three types of capacity?

(10)
,GSUNG RAB KUN GYI SNYING PO BSDU BSDU BA,
,TSUL 'DI THUN RE STON DANG NYAN PAS KYANG,
,DAM CHOS 'CHAD DANG THOS PA'I PHAN YON TSOGS,
,RLABS CHEN SDUD PAR NGES PAS DE DON BSAM,

This then is a system
Which embodies the
Deepest heart

Of all the high speech
Of the Enlightened Ones.

When we teach or listen
To the steps
Even just a single time,

We are able thus
To obtain,
With perfect certainty,
And with powerful efficiency,

All the benefits
Of explaining,
And listening to,
All the holy Dharma.

Contemplate then
This point well.

(11)
,DE NAS 'DI PHYI'I LEGS TSOGS JI SNYED PA'I,
,RTEN 'BREL LEGS PAR 'GRIG PA'I RTZA BA NI,
,LAM STON BSHES GNYEN DAM PA 'BAD PA YIS,
,BSAM DANG SBYOR BAS TSUL BZHIN BSTEN PA RU,

The specific root cause then
For getting off
To a good start

In the entire collection
Of the good things

That could ever happen
In this life,
Or in our future lives,

Is our holy spiritual friend,
The one who shows us
The path.

And then with great efforts
We need to rely
Upon that Lama

In our thoughts
And in our actual actions.

(12)
,MTHONG NAS SROG GI PHYIR YANG MI GTONG BAR,
,BKA' BZHIN SGRUB PA'I MCHOD PAS MNYES PAR BYED,
,RNAL 'BYOR NGAS KYANG NYAMS LEN DE LTAR BGYIS,
,THAR 'DOD KHYED KYANG DE BZHIN BSKYANG 'TSAL LO,

Seeing this,
We see that we must
Please them with the offering

Of accomplishing everything
They have commanded us to do,

Without ever giving it up,
Even at the cost of our life.

I, the deep practitioner,
Have accomplished my practice
This way;

And you who hope for freedom
Should do your practice
The same.

(13)
,DAL BA'I RTEN 'DI YID BZHIN NOR LAS LHAG
,'DI 'DRA RNYED PA DA RES TZAM ZHIG YIN,
,RNYED DKA' 'JIG SLA NAM MKHA'I GLOG DANG 'DRA,
,TSUL 'DI BSAMS NAS 'JIG RTEN BYA BA KUN,

This body & mind of leisure
Is more valuable than
A wishing jewel.

Our present life
Is the only one in which
We've been able
To find them.

It is hard to find,
And easily destroyed—
Like lightning in the sky.

Devoting some thought
To this, we need to realize

(14)
,SBUN PA 'PHYAR BA BZHIN DU RTOGS GYUR NAS,
,NYIN MTSAN KUN TU SNYING PO LEN PA DGOS,
,RNAL 'BYOR NGAS KYANG NYAMS LEN DE LTAR BGYIS,
,THAR 'DOD KHYED KYANG DE BZHIN BSKYANG 'TSAL LO,

That all our worldly activities
Are like the chaff we remove
From grains of wheat,

And spend every hour
Of the day & night
Working to get
The very essence
Out of it.

I, the deep practitioner,
Have accomplished my practice
This way;

And you who hope for freedom
Should do your practice
The same.

(15)
,SHI NAS NGAN 'GROR MI SKYE'I GDENG MED CING,
,DE YI 'JIGS SKYOB DKON MCHOG GSUM DU NGES,
,DE PHYIR SKYABS 'GRO SHIN TU BRTAN PA DANG,
,DE YI BSLAB BYA NYAMS PA MED PAR BYA,

I have no guarantee that,
Once I do die,
I won't have to take birth
Into the lower realms.

The only shelter
Which can protect us
From this terror is—
With absolute certainty—
The Three Jewels.

To that end,
We must make sure
That our act of

Taking shelter
Is steadfast.

And then we need
To assure that we
Never digress
In the advices.

(16)
,DE YANG DKAR NAG LAS 'BRAS LEGS BSAMS NAS,
,BLANG DOR TSUL BZHIN SGRUB LA RAG LAS SO,
,RNAL 'BYOR NGAS KYANG NYAMS LEN DE LTAR BGYIS,
,THAR 'DOD KHYED KYANG DE BZHIN BSKYANG 'TSAL LO,

And now we have to
Consider, carefully,
White & black karma,
And its consequences.

We have to rely
On a practice that
Relates in a correct way

To what we take up
And what we give up.
I, the deep practitioner,
Have accomplished my practice
This way;

And you who hope for freedom
Should do your practice
The same.

(17)
,LAM MCHOG SGRUB LA MTSAN NYID TSANG BA'I RTEN,
,MA RNYED BAR DU SA PHYOD {%CHOD} MI 'ONG [f. 56b] BAS,
,DE YI MA TSANG MED PA'I RGYU LA BSLAB,
,SGO GSUM SDIG LTUNG DRI MAS SPAGS [*SBAGS] PA 'DI,

If we hope to achieve
That supreme path,
Then we need to find

A body & mind
Which possesses the
Requisite qualities,
All complete.

Until we do,
We won't be able to take
Great bounds forward.

And so we need
To train ourselves
In the necessary causes,
In no way incomplete.

The fact is that
We have been dirtied
By the stain

Of negative actions
And downfalls

Committed through
The three doors of
Our actions, words, and thoughts.

(18)
,LHAG PAR LAS SGRIB SBYONG BA GNAD CHE BAS,
,RGYUN DU STOBS BZHI TSANG BAR BSTEN PA GCES,
,RNAL 'BYOR NGAS KYANG NYAMS LEN DE LTAR BGYIS,
,THAR 'DOD KHYED KYANG DE BZHIN BSKYANG 'TSAL LO,

The most crucial
Priority we have
Is to clean ourselves

Of the obstacles
We've created by
Our own karma.

As such,
We should learn to cherish
This method of
Depending constantly

Upon the practice
Where we employ
All four powers complete.

I, the deep practitioner,
Have accomplished my practice
This way;

And you who hope for freedom
Should do your practice
The same.

(19)
,SDUG BDEN NYES DMIGS BSAM LA MA 'BAD NA,
,THAR PA DON GNYER JI BZHIN MI SKYE ZHING,
,KUN 'BYUNG 'KHOR BA'I 'JUG RIM MA BSAMS NA,
,'KHOR BA'I RTZA BA GCOD TSUL MI SHES PAS,

If we don't make
Sincere efforts
In contemplating

The problems of
The truth of suffering,
Then we won't be able
To give birth

To a truly authentic form
Of the wish for freedom.

And suppose
We are unable
To contemplate, properly,

The various stages
In which the circle
Starts to turn:

The source
Of suffering.

We will never
Understand how to sever
The very root of the cycle of pain.

(20)
,SRID LAS NGES 'BYUNG SKYO SHAS BRTAN {%BSTEN} PA DANG,
,'KHOR BAR GANG GIS BCINGS PA SHES PA GCES,
,RNAL 'BYOR NGAS KYANG NYAMS LEN DE LTAR BGYIS,
,THAR 'DOD KHYED KYANG DE BZHIN BSKYANG 'TSAL LO,

We need to find
Within ourselves

Disgust and exhaustion
With this situation:

A strong desire
To escape from
This life of pain.
We need to treasure
The knowledge

Of what it is
That keeps us chained
To this cycle of pain.

I, the deep practitioner,

Have accomplished my practice
This way;

And you who hope for freedom
Should do your practice
The same.

(21)
,SEMS BSKYED THEG MCHOG LAM GYI GZHUNG SHING STE,
,RLABS CHEN SPYOD PA RNAMS KYI GZHI DANG RTEN,
,TSOGS GNYIS KUN LA GSER 'GYUR RTZI LTA BU,
,RAB 'BYAMS DGE TSOGS SDUD PA'I BSOD NAMS GTER,

The Wish for enlightenment
Is the main beam
That holds up the entire path
Of the supreme vehicle.

It is the foundation,
And the basis,
For vastly effective
Activities.

For everything about
The two collections
Of merit & wisdom,

The Wish is like
That alchemical elixir

Which turns things
Into gold.

It is a mine of merit
Which incorporates
Collections of
A myriad number
Of good deeds.

(22)
,DE LTAR SHES NAS RGYAL SRAS DPA' BO RNAMS,
,RIN CHEN SEMS MCHOG THUGS DAM MTHIL DU 'DZIN,
,RNAL 'BYOR NGAS KYANG NYAMS LEN DE LTAR BGYIS,
,THAR 'DOD KHYED KYANG DE BZHIN BSKYANG 'TSAL LO,

> Once they have
> Learned thus,
>
> The children of the Victors—
> The warriors—
>
> Make this supreme
> State of mind,
> This jewel,
>
> The spiritual centerpiece
> Of their practice.
>
> I, the deep practitioner,
> Have accomplished my practice
> This way;
>
> And you who hope for freedom
> Should do your practice
> The same.

(23)
,SBYIN PA 'GRO BA'I RE SKONG YID BZHIN NOR,
,SER SNA'I MDUD PA GCOD PA'I MTSON CHA MCHOG
,MA ZHUM SNYING STOBS BSKYED PA'I RGYAL SRAS SPYOD,
,SNYAN PA'I GRAGS PA PHYOGS BCUR SGROG PA'I GZHI,

> Giving is a wishing jewel
> Which fulfils the hopes
> Of living beings;
>
> It is a supreme blade
> For cutting

The knot of stinginess.

It is an activity
For children of the Victors
Which inspires within us

A kind of courage,
Where we are never
Hesitant;

And it serves as a basis
For the praises
Of our fame

To be proclaimed
In all the ten directions.

(24)
,DE LTAR SHES NAS LUS DANG LONGS SPYOD DGE
,YONGS SU GTONG BA'I LAM BZANG MKHAS PAS BSTEN,
,RNAL 'BYOR NGAS KYANG NYAMS LEN DE LTAR BGYIS,
,THAR 'DOD KHYED KYANG DE BZHIN BSKYANG 'TSAL LO,

Once they understand
How all this works,
Wise ones betake themselves
To this noble path,

Where they feel free
To give away their body,
The things that they possess,
And their goodness.

I, the deep practitioner,
Have accomplished my practice
This way;

And you who hope for freedom
Should do your practice

The same.

(25)
,TSUL KHRIMS NYES SPYOD DRI MA 'KHRUD PA'I CHU,
,NYON MONGS TSA GDUNG SEL BA'I ZLA BA'I 'OD,
,SKYE DGU'I DBUS NA LHUN PO LTA BUR BRJID,
,STOBS KYIS BSDIGS PA MED PAR 'GRO KUN 'DUD,

> The practice of leading
> An ethical life
>
> Is pure water
> Which washes away
> The stains of all
> Bad behavior.
>
> It is moonlight
> That clears away
> The torment of the heat
> Of negative emotions.
>
> It stands with majesty
> Among the crowds
> Of humankind,
> Like the central mountain.
>
> Due to its power,
> All beings bow down,
> And never think
> To threaten us.

(26)
,DE LTAR SHES NAS YANG DAG BLANGS PA'I KHRIMS,
,DAM PA RNAMS KYIS MIG BZHIN BSRUNG BAR MDZAD,
,RNAL 'BYOR NGAS KYANG NYAMS LEN DE LTAR BGYIS,
,THAR 'DOD KHYED KYANG DE BZHIN BSKYANG 'TSAL LO,

> Once we understand all this,
> We need to act

As the holy ones did,

Protecting the practice
Of a truly pure,
Ethical life

In the same way
That we instinctively
Shield our eyes.

I, the deep practitioner,
Have accomplished my practice
This way;

And you who hope for freedom
Should do your practice
The same.

(27)
,BZOD PA STOBS LDAN RNAMS LA RGYAN GYI MCHOG
,[f. 57a] NYON MONGS GDUNG BA'I DKA' THUB KUN GYI PHUL,
,ZHE SDANG LAG 'GRO'I DGRA LA NAM MKHA' LDING,
,TSIG RTZUB MTSON LA SRA BA'I GO CHA YIN,

Patience is the highest jewel
For those of true strength;

It is the very acme,
Or highest asceticism
Of all, for those
Tormented by
Negative emotions.

It is a skyglider
Against the enemy

Of the palm walker
Of anger.

And it is
Impenetrable armor
Against the
Spears & arrows
Of harsh words.

(28)
,DE LTAR SHES NAS BZOD MCHOG GO CHA LA,
,RNAM PA SNA TSOGS TSUL GYIS GOMS PAR MDZAD,
,RNAL 'BYOR NGAS KYANG NYAMS LEN DE LTAR BGYIS,
,THAR 'DOD KHYED KYANG DE BZHIN BSKYANG 'TSAL LO,

Once they realized this,
They undertook to
Accustom their hearts—

In a great variety
Of different ways—

To donning
Their own armor:
A supreme form
Of patience.

I, the deep practitioner,
Have accomplished my practice
This way;

And you who hope for freedom
Should do your practice
The same.

(29)
,MI LDOG {%BZLOG} BRTAN PA'I BRTZON 'GRUS GO BGOS NA,
,LUNG RTOGS YON TAN YAR NGO'I ZLA BZHIN 'PHEL,
,SPYOD LAM THAMS CAD DON DANG LDAN PAR 'GYUR,
,GANG BRTZAMS LAS KYI MTHA' RNAMS YID BZHIN 'GRUB,

Suppose we are able
To don the strong armor

Of steadfast, joyful effort,
Never turning back.

Our fine qualities—
In both scriptural study
And inner realizations—
Will multiply,
Like a waxing moon.

Any project we undertake
Will end up having
A meaningful result;

And any undertaking
We ever initiate
Will come to its
Successful conclusion,
Just as we intended.

(30)
,DE LTAR SHES NAS LE LO KUN SEL BA'I,
,RLABS CHEN BRTZON 'GRUS RGYAL SRAS RNAMS KYIS BRTZAMS,
,RNAL 'BYOR NGAS KYANG NYAMS LEN DE LTAR BGYIS,
,THAR 'DOD KHYED KYANG DE BZHIN BSKYANG 'TSAL LO,

Children of the Victors
Understood perfectly
These points,

And so they were
Able to undertake
Joyful effort which was
Hugely effective,

To clear away
Every trace
Of laziness.

I, the deep practitioner,
Have accomplished my practice
This way;

And you who hope for freedom
Should do your practice
The same.

(31)
,BSAM GTAN SEMS LA DBANG BSGYUR RGYAL PO STE,
,BZHAG NA G-YO MED RI YI DBANG PO BZHIN,
,BTANG NA DGE BA'I DMIGS PA KUN LA 'JUG
,LUS SEMS LAS SU RUNG BA'I BDE CHEN 'DREN,

Meditation is a king
Who enjoys total authority
Over the realm
Of their own mind.

When you place it
Upon an object,
It stays there

Completely immobile,
Like the king
Of all mountains.

And any time
You release this,
It moves off to
Every different kind
Of virtuous focus.

It always elicits

The great bliss
Where both body & mind
Are extremely flexible.

(32)
,DE LTAR SHES NAS RNAL 'BYOR DBANG PO RNAMS,
,RNAM G-YENG DGRA 'JOMS TING 'DZIN RGYUN DU BSTEN,
,RNAL 'BYOR NGAS KYANG NYAMS LEN DE LTAR BGYIS,
,THAR 'DOD KHYED KYANG DE BZHIN BSKYANG 'TSAL LO,

Armed with this understanding,
Lords among deep practitioners
Undertook the constant practice
Of focused meditation,

Where they destroyed
The enemy of distraction.

I, the deep practitioner,
Have accomplished my practice
This way;

And you who hope for freedom
Should do your practice
The same.

(33)
,SHES RAB ZAB MO'I DE NYID LTA BA'I MIG
,SRID PA'I RTZA BA DRUNGS NAS 'BYIN PA'I LAM,
,GSUNG RAB KUN LAS BSNGAGS PA'I YON TAN GTER,
,GTI MUG MUN SEL SGRON ME'I MCHOG TU GRAGS,

Wisdom is like
A pair of eyes
That allow us to view
Profound suchness.

It is a path
That enables us

To rip out the very root
Of this kind of life.

It is a great goldmine
Of all the fine
Personal qualities
So highly praised
In all of that highest
Of the spoken word.

It is renowned
As the supreme lamp,
Lighting up the darkness
Of our blind ignorance.

(34)
,DE LTAR SHES NAS THAR 'DOD MKHAS PA YIS,
,LAM DE 'BAD PA DU MAS BSKYED PAR MDZAD,
,RNAL 'BYOR NGAS KYANG NYAMS LEN DE LTAR BGYIS,
,THAR 'DOD KHYED KYANG DE BZHIN BSKYANG 'TSAL LO,

Once they understand all this,
Wise ones who seek for freedom
Make a great many efforts
In this path, undertaking
To produce it.
I, the deep practitioner,
Have accomplished my practice
This way;

And you who hope for freedom
Should do your practice
The same.

(35)
,RTZE GCIG BSAM GTAN TZAM LA 'KHOR BA YI,
,RTZA BA GCOD PA'I NUS PA MA MTHONG ZHING,
,ZHI GNAS LAM DANG BRAL BA'I SHES RAB KYIS,
,JI TZAM DPYAD KYANG NYON MONGS MI LDOG PAS,

We can't see that
Single-pointed meditation
Would possess, by itself,

Sufficient power
To sever the root
Of the cycle of pain.

We can use wisdom
Divorced from the path
Of quietude to perform as much
Examination as we want,

But still we will find ourselves
Unable to put a stop
To our negative emotions.

(36)
,YIN LUGS PHU THAG CHOD PA'I SHES RAB DE,
,G-YO MED ZHI GNAS RTA LA BSKYON NAS NI,
,MTHA' [f. 57b] BRAL DBU MA'I RIGS PA'I MTSON RNON GYIS,
,MTHAR 'DZIN DMIGS GTOD THAMS CAD 'JIG BYED PA'I,

They took a form of wisdom
Which was able to delve
Down to how things
Really are,

And mounted it upon
The steed of quietude,
Which remains unmoved.

So they took up the razor sword
Of the reasoning of
The middle way,
Free of extremes—

Which allowed them to destroy

All of them, for their habit
Of holding to things
In an extreme way.

(37)
,TSUL BZHIN DPYOD PA'I YANGS PA'I SHES RAB KYIS,
,DE NYID RTOGS PA'I BLO GROS RGYAS PAR MDZAD,
,RNAL 'BYOR NGAS KYANG NYAMS LEN DE LTAR BGYIS,
,THAR 'DOD KHYED KYANG DE BZHIN BSKYANG 'TSAL LO,

They found a vast form of wisdom
That performed its analysis
With total accuracy,

And were able to expand
That high intelligence which
Allowed them to realize suchness.

I, the deep practitioner,
Have accomplished my practice
This way;

And you who hope for freedom
Should do your practice
The same.

(38)
,RTZE GCIG GOMS PAS TING 'DZIN 'GRUB PA NI,
,SMOS PAR CI 'TSAL TSUL BZHIN DPYOD PA YI,
,SO SOR RTOG PA YIS KYANG YIN LUGS LA,
,G-YO MED SHIN TU BRTAN PAR GNAS PA YI,

What need to mention
Accustoming ourselves
To remaining single-pointed,

And reaching
One-point concentration?
We then move into

Specific individual understandings,
Through accurate analysis.

Through this, we see
That we can give birth
To a fixed concentration

That can remain,
Very solidly
And without shifting,
On the way things
Really are.

(39)
,TING 'DZIN BSKYED PAR MTHONG NAS ZHE {%ZHI} LHAG GNYIS,
,ZUNG 'BREL SGRUB LA BRTZON RNAMS YA MTSAN NO,
,RNAL 'BYOR NGAS KYANG NYAMS LEN DE LTAR BGYIS,
,THAR 'DOD KHYED KYANG DE BZHIN BSKYANG 'TSAL LO,

Those who make intense efforts
Towards achieving the two
Of quietude & special insight
In combination
Are truly wondrous.

I, the deep practitioner,
Have accomplished my practice
This way;

And you who hope for freedom
Should do your practice
The same.

(40)
,MNYAM GZHAG NAM MKHA' LTA BU'I STONG NYID DANG,
,RJES THOB SGYU MA LTA BU'I STONG PA GNYIS,
,BSGOMS NAS THABS SHES ZUNG DU 'BREL BA YIS,
,RGYAL SRAS SPYOD PA'I PHA ROL 'GRO BAR BSNGAGS,

We continue to meditate
Upon these two:

Emptiness which is like
Empty space,
In a balanced meditation;

And then emptiness
In this aftermath,
Where things are
Like an illusion.

This is highly praised
As a journey to the far side
Of the activities

Of the children
Of the Victors;
Through a combination
Of the two
Of method & wisdom.

(41)
,DE LTAR RTOGS NAS PHYOGS RE'I LAM GYIS NI,
,TSIM PA MED PA SKAL BZANG RNAMS KYI LUGS,
,RNAL 'BYOR NGAS KYANG NYAMS LEN DE LTAR BGYIS,
,THAR 'DOD KHYED KYANG DE BZHIN BSKYANG 'TSAL LO,

Having come to this realization,
It is the way of those
Who have within them
Rich power of good deeds
To never be satisfied
With a path consisting of
Only either one of the pair.
I, the deep practitioner,
Have accomplished my practice

This way;

And you who hope for freedom
Should do your practice
The same.

(42)
,DE LTAR RGYU DANG 'BRAS BU'I THEG CHEN GYI,
,LAM MCHOG GNYIS KAR DGOS PA'I THUN MONG LAM,
,JI BZHIN BSKYED NAS MKHAS PA'I DED DPON GYI,
,MGON LA BRTEN NAS RGYUD SDE'I RGYA MTSO CHER,

That kind is a pathway
That is shared:

One which is necessary
For both of these
Supreme paths
Within the greater way:

That of the causes,
And also of the results.

We give birth to it
In exactly the right way;

And with that,
We must take ourselves
To someone who becomes
Our savior:

A ship captain
Who is a master.

We set off with them
Across the vast sea
Of the secret teachings.

(43)
,ZHUGS NAS YONGS RDZOGS MAN NGAG BSTEN PA DES,
,DAL 'BYOR THOB PA DON DANG LDAN PAR BYAS,
,RNAL 'BYOR NGAS KYANG NYAMS LEN DE LTAR BGYIS,
,THAR 'DOD KHYOD KYANG DE BZHIN BSKYANG 'TSAL LO,

> We become
> One of those people
> Who is able to
> Surrender themselves
>
> To these private advices,
> Which contain
> The absolute entirety.
>
> With this,
> We have truly
> Given some meaning
> To the fact that
> We came into this life
> With all the different
> Leisures & fortunes.
>
> I, the deep practitioner,
> Have accomplished my practice
> This way;
>
> And you who hope for freedom
> Should do your practice
> The same.

(44)
,RANG GI YID LA GOMS PAR BYA PHYIR DANG,
,SKAL BZANG GZHAN LA'ANG PHAN PAR BYA BA'I PHYIR,
,RGYAL BA DGYES PA'I YONGS SU RDZOGS PA'I LAM,
,GO SLA'I NGAG GIS BSHAD PA'I DGE BA DES,

> In order to accustom
> My mind to it,

184

And also to provide
My help to others
Who truly possess

Enough good karma,
Within them,

I have presented
This explanation

Of the complete entirety
Of the path which has pleased
The Victors themselves,

In wording
Quite easy to comprehend.

(45)
,'GRO BA KUN KYANG RNAM DAG LAM BZANG DANG,
,'BRAL MED GYUR CIG CES NA {%NI} SMON LAM 'DEBS,
,RNAL 'BYOR NGAS KYANG [f. 58a] SMON LAM DE LTAR BTAB,
,THAR 'DOD KHYED KYANG DE BZHIN 'DEBS 'TSAL LO,

And I make a solemn prayer that,
By this good karma
Which I have collected,

Each & every
Living being there is

May never be separated
From this pure
And beautiful path.

I, the deep practitioner,
Have made my prayers this way;
And you who hope for freedom
Should make your prayers the same.

,ZHES BYANG CHUB LAM GYI RIM PA'I NYAMS LEN GYI RNAM
GZHAG MDOR BSDUS TE BRJED BYANG DU BYAS PA 'DI NI, MANG
DU THOS PA'I DGE SLONG SPONG BA PA BLO BZANG GRAGS PA'I
DPAL GYIS, ,'BROG RI BO CHE DGE LDAN RNAM PAR RGYAL BA'I
GLING DU SBYAR BA'O,, ,,

This then is a brief presentation on how to put into
practice the various steps of the path to enlightenment,
written out to help me remember all the points. It has
been composed by a very learned monk who has given
up the world: by the glorious [Je Tsongkapa,] Lobsang
Drakpa. The work was completed at the monastery
known as Ganden, land of goodness, isle of the final
victory, nestled below Shepherd's Peak.

An outline of the text

I. SNGON 'GRO MCHOD BRJOD SOGS, [f. 1b]
Preliminary steps such as the offering of praise and so forth

A. MCHOD PAR BRJOD PA, [f. 1b]
The offering of praise

1. ['JAM DPAL DBYANGS LA PHYAG 'TSAL BA,]
[f. 1b, prostration to Gentle Voice]
Prostration to Gentle Voice

2. [MCHOD BRJOD DNGOS,] [f. 1b]
The actual offering of praise

a. THUB DBANG LA PHYAG 'TSALBA,
[f. 1b, v. 1]
Bowing to the Lord of the Able Ones

b. [RJE BTZUN BYAMS PA DANG 'JAM DPAL LA
PHYAG 'TSAL BA,]
[f. 2a, v. 2]
Bowing down to Maitreya and Manjushri

c. [SHING RTA'I SROL 'BYED GNYIS LA
PHYAG 'TSAL BA,] [f. 2b, v. 3]
Bowing down to the two innovators

d. [MAR ME MDZAD LA PHYAG 'TSAL BA,]
[f. 2b, v. 4]
Bowing down to Lord Atisha

e. [BSHES GNYEN RNAMS LA
PHYAG 'TSAL BA,] [f. 2b, v. 5]
Bowing to all spiritual friends

B. BSHAD BYA NGOS BZUNG BA, [f. 3a]
An identification of what it is we will be explaining

   1. BRGYUD PA'I KHYAD PAR, [f. 3a, v. 6]
   A feature of the lineage

   2. KHYAD CHOS, [f. 3a]
   Specific other features

      a. DPE DON GYI KHYAD PAR,
         [f. 3a, v. 7]
      Specific metaphors and their intent

      b. KHYAD CHOS DNGOS,
         [f. 3b, v. 8]
      The actual features

   3. DGOS PA, [f. 4a]
   The purpose

      a. CHE BA DE LDAN GYI CHOS 'DI NYAMS
         SU LEN RIGS PA, [f. 4a, v. 9]
      Showing how appropriate it is then
         to put into practice this teaching, with
         its different types of greatness

      b. NYAMS SU BLANGS PA'I
         PHAN YON, [f. 4a, v. 10]
      The benefits we receive from
         putting things into actual practice this
         way

II. DNGOS GZHI GZHUNG DON, [f. 4a]
The meaning of the actual text of the work

   A. THUN MONG BA'I LAM LA BSLAB TSUL,
      [f. 4a]
   An explanation of how we practice the path
     of the shared steps

      1. SNGON 'GRO, [f. 4a, vv. 11-12]
      The preliminaries

2. DNGOS GZHI, [f. 4b]
The actual instruction

    a. DAL 'BYOR LA SNYING PO LEN
        PAR BSKUL BA, [f. 4b, v. 13a]
    Strong advice that we try to get the
        very essence out of the leisure & fortune
        that we have

    b. SNYING PO JI LTAR LEN TSUL,
        [f. 5a]
    Just how we derive this essence

        i. LAM GYI DBANG DU BYAS PA'I GSUNG RAB
            RNAMS 'DU TSUL,
            [f. 5a]
        How we group the high teachings
            with regard to the path

        ii. NYAMS SU LEN TSUL DNGOS,
            [f. 5b]
        The actual way in which we go
            about deriving the essence mentioned

        a2) SKYES BU CHUNG NGU
            DANG THUN MONG BA'I LAM, [f. 5b]
        The path which is shared with
            those of lesser capacity

        a3) PHYI MA DON GNYER GYI
            BLO BSKYED PA, [f. 5b]
        Giving birth to the state of
            mind where we are aspiring to
            goals that will come after we die

        a4) 'CHI BA MI RTAG PA BSAM PA,
            [f. 5b, vv. 13b-14]
        The contemplation on
            our impermanence,
            in the form of our death

        b4) NGAN 'GRO'I
            SDUG BSNGALBSAM PA,

[f. 5b, v. 15a]
The contemplation upon
    the sufferings of the lower realms

b3) PHYI MA'I BDE THABS
    BSTEN PA, [f. 5b]
How to engage in methods
    that will bring us happiness
    after this death

a4) SKYABS 'GRO BSLAB BYA
    DANG BCAS PA,
    [f. 5b, v. 15b]
An explanation of how to
    go for shelter, along
    with the traditional
    advices for this practice

b4) DE LA LAS GNYIS KYI BLANG
    DOR LA 'JUG DGOS PA,
    [f. 6a, v. 16]
An explanation of how,
    in this regard, we will need
    to learn to take up and give
    up, respectively, the two
    kinds of karma

c4) RNAM MKHYEN SGRUB
    PA'I RTEN BSHAD PA,
    [f. 6a]
A presentation on the foundation
    that we need to lay, in
    order to achieve the
    state of omniscience

a5) BSHAD PA DNGOS,
    [f. 6a, v. 17a]
The actual presentation

b5) STOBS BZHI BSTEN TSUL,
    [f. 6b, vv. 17b-18]
A description of how we

use the four powers

b2) SKYES BU 'BRING DANG THUN
     MONG BA'I LAM, [f. 6b]
The path which is shared with those of
     medium capacity

a3) SDUG KUN GNYIS KYI NYES
     DMIGS PA BSAM DGOS
     PA'I RGYU MTSAN,
     [f. 6b, v. 20a]
An explanation of the reasons
     why we should contemplate
     the problems of the two
     truths of suffering
     and its source

b3) BSAM TSUL DNGOS, [f. 7a, v. 20b]
The actual method for
     engaging in
     this contemplation

c2) SKYES BU CHEN PO'I LAM DNGOS,
     [f. 7b]
The actual path for people
     of greater capacity

a3) SPYOD PA'I RTEN SEMS
     BSKYED, [f. 7b]
The Wish for enlightenment which
     is the basis for the activities
     of a bodhisattva

a4) SEMS BSKYED KYI
     KHYAD CHOS SAM PHAN
     YON, [f. 7b, v. 21]
A list of the features,
     or benefits, of the Wish
b4) SEMS BSKYED BSKYED
     TSUL, [f. 7b, v. 22]
The method for developing the Wish

b3) SPYOD PA LA BSLAB TSUL, [f. 7b]
Instructions for training

ourselves in these activities

a4) SBYIN PA, [f. 7b]
Giving

  a5) KHYAD CHOS
      SAM PHAN YON,
      [f. 7b, v. 23]
  Features, or benefits

  b5) GTONG TSUL,
      [f. 8a, v. 24]
  The method we follow
      to perform giving

b4) TSUL KHRIMS, [f. 8a]
The ethical life

  a5) KHYAD CHOS
      SAM PHAN YON,
      [f. 8a, v. 25]
  Features, or benefits

  b5) SRUNG TSUL,
      [f. 8a, v. 26]
  The method we follow
      to honor the ethical life

c4) BZOD PA, [f. 8a]
Patience

  a5) KHYAD CHOS SAM PHAN
      YON, [f. 8a, v. 27]
  Features, or benefits

  b5) BSGOM TSUL,
      [f. 8b, v. 28]
  The method we follow
      to keep our patience

d4) BRTZON 'GRUS, [f. 8b]
Joyful effort

  a5) KHYAD CHOS SAM

PHAN YON, [f. 8b, v. 29]
Features, or benefits

b5) RTZOM TSUL,
[f. 8b, v. 30]
The method we follow
to undertake joyful effort

e4) BSAM GTAN, [f. 8b]
Meditation

a5) KHYAD CHOS SAM
PHAN YON, [f. 8b, v. 31]
Features, or benefits

b5) BSGOM TSUL,
[f. 8b, v. 32]
The method we follow
to practice meditation

f4) SHES RAB [f. 9a]
Wisdom

a5) SHES RAB BSGOM TSUL,
[f. 9a]
How to meditate upon wisdom

a6) KHYAD CHOS SAM
PHAN YON, [f. 9a, v. 33]
Features, or benefits

b6) BSGOM TSUL, [f. 9a, v. 34]
The method we follow
to perform the meditation
on wisdom

b5) ZHI LHAG ZUNG DU
'BREL TSUL, [f. 9a]
How to combine quietude &
special insight
into a single unit

a6) ZHI LHAG

ZUNG 'BREL
BSGOM PA'I
DGOS PA,
[f. 9a, vv. 35, 36, 37]
An explanation of why
we need to meditate
upon quietude & special
insight combined
into a single unit

b6) BSGOM TSUL DNGOS
[f. 9b, vv. 38, 39]
The actual instructions
for this particular type
of meditation

c5) MNYAM RJES GNYIS
KA SKYONG TSUL
YAN LAG DANG
BCAS PA, [f. 9b, vv. 40, 41]
How to conduct both periods
of a session—both
balanced meditation
and the aftermath period,
along with some
ancillary points

B. THUN MONG MA YIN PA'I LAM LA BSLAB TSUL,
[f. 10a, vv. 42, 43]
An explanation of how we practice the path of the
unique steps

III. MJUG GI BSHAD PA'I KHYAD PAR,
[f. 10a, vv. 44, 45, colophon]
Details of closing section of the composition.

Bibliography

**Bibliography of works
originally written in Sanskrit**

*Note that an asterisk (*) indicates that we have reconstructed
a name or term.*

S1
Candrakīrti (Tib: Zla-ba grags-pa), c. 650AD. *Seventy
Verses on Going for Shelter to the Three (Triśaraṇa Gamana
Saptati)* (Tib: *gSum la skyabs su 'gro-ba bdun-cu-pa*, Tibetan
translation at ACIP TD03971, ff. 251a-253b of Vol. 17 [*Gi*]
in the Middle-Way Section [*Madhyāmaka, dBu-ma*] of the
bsTan-'gyur [*sDe-dge* edition]).

S2
Nāgārjuna (Tib: Klu-sgrub), c. 200AD. *The String of
Precious Jewels, Words Offered to the King (Rāja Parikathā
Ratna Mālī)* (Tib: *rGyal-po la gtam-bya-ba Rin-po-che'i
phreng-ba*, Tibetan translation at ACIP TD04158, ff.
107a-126a of Vol. 93 [*Ge*] in the Epistles Section [*Lekha,
sPring-yig*] of the *bsTan-'gyur* [*sDe-dge* edition]).

S3
Maitreya (Tib: Byams-pa), as dictated to Asaṅga (Tib:
Thogs-med), c. 350AD. *The Jewel of Realizations, a Book of
Advices upon the Perfection of Wisdom (Abhisamayālaṅkāra
Nāma Prajñāpāramitopadeśa Śāstra)* (Tib: *Shes-rab kyi pha-
rol tu phyin-pa'i man-ngag gi bstan-bcos mNgon-par rtogs-
pa'i rgyan*, Tibetan translation at ACIP TD03786, ff. 1b-13a

of Vol. 1 [*Ka*] in the Perfection of Wisdom Section [*Prajñā Pāramitā, Shes-phyin*] of the *bsTan-'gyur* [*sDe-dge* edition]).

S4

Ratnākaraśanta* (Tib: Rin-chen 'byung-gnas zhi-ba), @. *The Jewel of the Shining Gem, a Commentary to [Arya Nagarjuna's] Compendium of the Sutras (Sūtra Samucchayālaṃkāra Bhāṣya Ratnāloka)* (Tib: *mDo kun las btus-pa'i bshad-pa Rin-po-che snang-ba'i rgyan,* Tibetan translation at ACIP TD03935, ff. 215a-334a of Vol. 15 [*Ki*] in the Middle-Way Section [*Madhyāmaka, dBu-ma*] of the *bsTan-'gyur* [*sDe-dge* edition]).

S5

Śākyamuni Buddha (Tib: Sh'akya thub-pa), 500BC. *The Perfection of Wisdom in 25,000 Lines (Pañca Viṃśati Sāhasrikā Prajñā Pāramitā)* (Tib: *Shes-rab kyi pha-rol tu phyin-pa stong-phrag nyi-shu lnga-pa,* Tibetan translation at ACIP KL00009, in three parts: ff. 1b-558a of Vol. 1 [*Ka*]; ff. 1b-548a of Vol. 2 [*Kha*]; and ff. 1b-537a of Vol. 3 [*Ga*] in the Perfection of Wisdom in 25,000 Lines Section [*Pañca Vimśati Sāhasrikā, Nyi-khri*] of the *bKa'-'gyur* [*lHa-sa* edition]).

Bibliography of works originally written in Tibetan

B1

(Gung-thang) dKon-mchog bstan-pa'i sgron-me (1762-1823). *Notes to a Teaching on the "Thousand Angels of the Heaven of Bliss, a Lama Practice" (Bla-ma'i rnal-'byor dGa'-ldan lha-brgya'i khrid kyi zin-bris,* ACIP S00930), ff. 1a-10a.

B2

(Co-ne bla-ma) Grags-pa bshad-sgrub, 1675-1748. *Easy to Use & Helpful to All: A Dissection Presentation of the Steps on the Path to Enlightenment (Byang-chub lam gyi rim-pa'i dmar-'khrid 'Khyer-bde kun-phan* ACIP S25235), ff. 1a-22a

B3

(Co-ne bla-ma) Grags-pa bshad-sgrub, 1675-1748. *A Brief Clarification of Heart: A Word-by-Word Commentary to "An Abbreviated Presentation of the Steps to the Path" (Lam-rim bsdus-don gyi tsig-'grel snying-po mdor-bsdus gsal-ba,* ACIP S00184), ff. 1a-11a.

B4

(T'a-la'i sku-phreng lnga-pa, lNga-pa chen-po, rGyal-ba) lNga-pa chen-po Ngag-dbang blo-bzang rgya-mtso, 1617-1682. *The Word of Gentle Voice: A Guide Book for the Steps on the Path to Enlightenment (Byang-chub lam gyi rim-pa'i 'khrid-yig 'Jam-pa'i dbyangs kyi zhal-lung,* ACIP S05637), ff. 1a-95a.

B5

('Jam-dbyangs bzhad-pa sku-phreng dang-po) 'Jam-dbyangs bzhad-pa'i rdo-rje Ngag-dbang brtzon-'grus, 1648-1721. *The Jewel Lamp which Illuminates every Meaning of the Perfection of Wisdom: A Dialectical Analysis of the Classical Commentary known as the "Jewel of Realizations" (bsTan-bcos mngon-par rtogs-pa'i rgyan gyi mtha'-dpyod Shes-rab kyi pha-rol tu phyin-pa'i don kun gsal-ba'i rin-chen sgron-me,* ACIP S19088), ff. 1a-290a.

B6

('Jam-dbyangs bzhad-pa sku-phreng dang-po) 'Jam-dbyangs bzhad-pa'i rdo-rje Ngag-dbang brtzon-'grus, 1648-1721. *The Lineage Words of the Lama: A Practical Way of Carrying Out the Brief Essence of "The Word of Gentle Voice," a Dissection Presentation on the Steps of the Path to Enlightenment* (Byang-chub lam gyi rim-pa'i dmar-khrid 'Jam-dpal zhal-lung gi snying-po bsdus-pa'i nyams-len 'khyer-bde Bla-ma'i gsung-rgyun, ACIP S19061), ff. 1a-51a.

B7

('Jam-dbyangs bzhad-pa sku-phreng dang-po) 'Jam-dbyangs bzhad-pa'i rdo-rje Ngag-dbang brtzon-'grus, 1648-1721. Oral teaching transcribed by Ngag-dbang blo-bzang. *A Dissection Presentation Related to the Lama Practice called 'The Thousand Angels of the Heaven of Bliss,' along with Private Instructions* (Bla-ma'i rnal-'byor dGa'-ldan lha-brgya-ma dang 'brel-ba'i dmar-khrid zhal-shes dang bcas-pa, ACIP S19001), ff. 1a-6a.

B8

rJe Tzong-kha-pa (Blo-bzang grags-pa), 1357-1419. *The Great Book on the Steps of the Path, Composed by the Great One, the Incomparable Tsongkapa* (mNyam-med Tzong-kha-pa chen-pos mdzad-pa'i Byang-chub lam-rim che-ba, ACIP S05392L), ff. 1a-523a.

B9

rJe Tzong-kha-pa (Blo-bzang grags-pa), 1357-1419. *The Essence of Well-Spoken Words: A Praise of the Unsurpassed Teacher for His Having Spoken the Profound Teachings on Creation in Dependence* (sTon-pa bla-na-med-pa la zab-mo rten cing 'brel-par 'byung-ba gsung-ba'i sgo nas bstod-pa Legs-par bshad-pa'i snying-po, ACIP S05275-15), ff. 13a-16a.

B10

rJe Tzong-kha-pa Blo-bzang grags-pa, 1357-1419. *A*

Brief Presentation of the Practice of the Steps of the Path to Buddhahood, composed in the Form of Notes (*Byang-chub lam gyi rim-pa'i nyams-len gyi rnam-gzhag mdor-bsdus te brjed-byang du byas-pa*, ACIP S05275-59), ff. 55b-58a. Also known as *Lam-rim bsdus-don* (*An Abbreviated Presentation of the Steps to the Path*) or, alternately, *rJe Rin-po-che'i nyams-mgur* (*Je Tsongkapa's "Song of My Spiritual Life"*).

Note that historically the catalog number for the text has also sometimes been given in the ACIP database as S05275-57. This is due to numbering differences for Je Tsongkapa's "miscellaneous" works, all listed under S05275.

B11

(mKhas-grub) bsTan-pa dar-rgyas, 1493-1568. *An Illumination of the "Jewel of the Essence of Good Explanation" — an Overview of the Root Text and Commentary to the Classical Commentary known as the "Jewel of Realizations"* (*bsTan-bcos mNgon-par rtogs-pa'i rgyan rtza-'grel gyi spyi-don rNam-bshad snying-po rgyan gyi snang-ba phar-phyin spyi-don*, ACIP S00009), in 6 volumes: Vol. 1 (commentary to the first chapter), ACIP SL00009N1, ff. 1a-141a; Vol. 2 (second chapter), ACIP S00009M2, ff. 1a-37a; Vol. 3 (third chapter), ACIP S00009M3, ff. 1a-15a; Vol. 4 (fourth chapter), ACIP S00009M4, ff. 1a-65a; Vol. 5 (fifth through seventh chapters), ACIP S00009M5, ff. 1a-21a; and Vol. 6 (eighth chapter), ACIP S00009M6, ff. 1a-24a.

B12

Pha-bong kha-pa bDe-chen snying-po, 1878-1941, oral teachings edited by sKyabs-rje Khri-byang rin-po-che (Blo-bzang ye-shes bstan-'dzin rgya-mtso), 1901-1981. *"A Gift of Liberation, Thrust into the Palm of Your Hand; the Heart of the Nectar of Holy Advices; the Very Essence of All the Highest of Spoken Words," representing Profound, Complete, and Unerring Instruction taken down as Notes during a Teaching, of the Kind Based on Personal Experience, upon*

*the Steps of the Path to Enlightenment, the Heart-Essence of
the Incomparable King of the Dharma (rNam-grol lag bcangs
su gtod-pa'i man-ngag zab-mo tsang la ma-nor-ba mtsungs-
med chos kyi rgyal-po'i thugs-bcud byang-chub lam gyi rim-
pa'i nyams-khrid kyi zin-bris gsung-rab kun gyi bcud-bsdus
gdams-ngag bdud-rtzi'i snying-po Lam-rim rnam-grol lag-
bcangs,* ACIP S00004), ff. 1a-392a.

B13

(Paṇ-chen sku-phreng dang-po) Blo-bzang chos kyi rgyal-
mtsan, 1565-1662. *The Path of Bliss, for Travelling to the
State of Knowing All Things: Instructions, in the "Dissection"
Format, on the Steps of the Path to Enlightenment (Byang-
chub lam gyi rim-pa'i dmar-khrid Thams-cad mkhyen-par
bgrod-pa'i bde-lam,* ACIP S05944), ff. 1a-33a.

B14

(mKhas-grub) sByin-pa dar-rgyas, b. 1558. *The Jewel
Necklace for Intelligent Young Minds: An Overview of the
Subject of the Turning of the Wheel of the Dharma Written by
the Wise & Accomplished Jinpa Dargye (mKhas-grub sByin-
pa dar-rgyas kyis mdzad-pa'i chos-'khor gyi spyi-don Blo-gsal
gzhon-nu'i mgrin-rgyan,* ACIP S00208), ff. 1a-27b.

B15

sNa-tsogs (various authors). *A Compendium of Liturgical
Texts Utilized at the Various Major Monasteries, along with
Liturgical Works which are Unique to Sera Mey Monastery
and Needed for Use by Its Members (Chos-sde chen-po rnams
su gsungs-pa'i chos-spyod kyi rim-pa dang Ser-smad thos-
bsam nor-gling grva-tsang gi thun-mong-ma-yin-pa'i nye-
mkho chos-spyod bcas,* ACIP S00207), ff. 1a-228a.

B16

Various authors, modern. *The Great Dictionary of the
Tibetan and Chinese Languages (Bod-rgya tsig-mdzod chen-
mo)* (Beijing: Mi-rigs dpe-skrun khang, 1985, ACIP
R00002), 3 vols.

Bibliography of works in English

E1

Pabongka Rinpoche, 1878-1941, edited by Kyabje Trijang Rinpoche (1901-1981). Translated by Khen Rinpoche Geshe Lobsang Tharchin (1921-2004) with Dr. Artemus B. Engle (b. 1948). *Liberation in Our Hands: A Series of Oral Discourses,* in three volumes: *Part I, The Preliminaries* (328pp); *Part II, The Fundamentals* (405pp); *Part III, The Ultimate Goals* (394pp). English translation of *Lam-rim rnam-grol lag-bcangs* (Howell, New Jersey: MSTP Press, 1999, 1994, 2001).

E2

Trichen Tenpa Rabgye, 1759-1815, commenting upon the root text of Dharma Rakshita (c. 1020AD), with notes by Gyalwang Trinley Namgyal (fl. 1825). Translated by Seiji Arao Takahashi with Geshe Michael Roach. *Deathless Nectar for Helping Others: Notes to a Teaching on the "Crown of Knives,"* English translation of *Khyab-bdag rDo-rje-'chang chen-po nas Blo-sbyong mtson-cha 'khor-lo'i bshad-lung stzal skabs kyi gsung-bshad zin-bris gZhan-phan my-gu bskyed-pa'i bdud-rtzi* (Sedona: Diamond Cutter Press, 2024). 855pp in manuscript, Volume 98 of the Diamond Cutter Classics Series.

The Diamond Cutter Classics Series

The book you are reading is one of over 100 volumes in the Diamond Cutter Classics Series. For those who are interested in furthering their study of the great ideas of ancient Asia, we provide the following list of titles in the series. They cover both original translations of the ancient classics; courses for modern life based upon them; and popular titles conveying the same information to a more general audience.

The titles in Group 5 marked with an asterisk (*) are completed and published, as of January 2024; printed and ebook versions are available from online booksellers worldwide, such as Amazon, as well as from the Diamond Cutter Press at *DiamondCutterPress.com*.

For more information, to follow the translation of these great books live, or to make any inquiry about our work, please visit the Diamond Cutter Classics Series website at *DiamondCutterClassics.com*. We would love to hear from you.

List of Titles

Group 1
Worldview Books for the Modern World

Volume 1
The Diamond Cutter:
The Buddha on Managing Your Business and Your Life

Volume 2
The Garden: A Parable

Volume 3
How Yoga Works

Volume 4
The Karma of Love:
100 Answers for Your Relationship

Volume 5
Karmic Management:
What Goes Around Comes Around,
in Your Business and Your Life

Volume 6
The Tibetan Book of Yoga:
Ancient Buddhist Teachings
on the Philosophy & Practice of Yoga

Volume 7
To the Inner Kingdom
Quiet Retreat Teachings Series, Book 1

Volume 8
The Magic of Empty Teachers
Quiet Retreat Teachings Series, Book 2

Volume 9
Second Sight
Quiet Retreat Teachings Series, Book 3

Volume 10
Ripples of Light
Quiet Retreat Teachings Series, Book 4

Volume 11
The Essential Yoga Sutra

Volume 12
King of the Dharma: The Illustrated Life of Je Tsongkapa

Volume 13
China Love You: The Death of Global Competition

Volume 14
The 10 Biggest Mistakes
You Can Make in Your Life (And How Not To)

Volume 15
The Eastern Path to Heaven:
A Guide to Happiness from the Teachings of Jesus in Tibet

Volume 16
A Better History of Time:
Ancient Answers to the Unsolved Riddles of Modern Science

Volume 17
If This Happens, That Happens: A Study of the Wheel of Life

Volume 18
Katrin: Girls Do Do That

Volume 19
Teachings from 3-Year Retreat

Volume 130
A Springtime Song of the Colorless Light

Volume 131
Outline for Saving a Civilization

Volume 134
My Desert Family:
Notes from 1,000 Circle Days

Group 2
Foundation Books
of the Diamond Cutter Institute (DCI)

Volume 20
DCI Foundation Book 1
Success Inside, Success Outside

Volume 21
DCI Foundation Book 2
Talent, Passion, Purpose:
Finding out What You're Supposed to Do in this World

Volume 22
DCI Foundation Book 3
Mastering Your Mind
for Success at Work and at Home

Volume 23
DCI Foundation Book 4
Finding, Keeping, and Loving Them:
The Karmic Secret to Great Relationships

Volume 24
DCI Foundation Book 5
12 Deeper Tools for Perfect Relationships
at Home & at Work

Volume 25
DCI Foundation Book 6
Peeling Off Our Addictions with the Wheel of Life

Volume 26
DCI Foundation Book 7
Reaching the Diamond World:
Learning to Touch the Source of All Success

Volume 27
DCI Foundation Book 8
Automatic Leadership

Volume 28
DCI Foundation Book 9
True Innovators:
The Deeper Causes of Creativity

Volume 29
DCI Foundation Book 10
Impossible Anger:
Never Get Upset Again

Volume 30
DCI Foundation Book 11
Time Management:
Using the Inner Conversation

Volume 31
DCI Foundation Book 12
The Art of Gratitude

Group 2
Advanced Books
of the Diamond Cutter Institute (DCI)

Volume 32
DCI Advanced Book 1
Problem-Solving Masterpieces

Volume 33
DCI Advanced Book 2
Techniques for Moving Dreams into Reality

Volume 34
DCI Advanced Book 3
Time to Upgrade:
Belief System Checklist for Success

Volume 35
DCI Advanced Book 4
Double Your Productivity
with Daily Wisdom AI

Volume 35
DCI Advanced Book 5
Enjoyable:
Fun (Deep) Tips for Enjoying Your Life More

Group 4
Foundation Books of
the Asian Classics Institute (ACI)
(all translated compilations from ancient classics)

Volume 36
ACI Foundation Book 1
The Principal Teachings of Buddhism

Volume 46
ACI Foundation Book 11
Guide to the Bodhisattva's Way of Life, Part II

Volume 47
ACI Foundation Book 12
Guide to the Bodhisattva's Way of Life, Part III

Volume 48
ACI Foundation Book 13
The Art of Reasoning

Volume 49
ACI Foundation Book 14
Lojong, Developing the Good Heart

Volume 50
ACI Foundation Book 15
What the Buddha Really Meant

Volume 51
ACI Foundation Book 16
The Great Ideas of Buddhism, Part One
A Review of ACI Courses 1–5

Volume 52
ACI Foundation Book 17
The Great Ideas of Buddhism, Part Two
A Review of ACI Courses 6–10

Volume 53
ACI Foundation Book 18
The Great Ideas of Buddhism, Part Three
A Review of ACI Courses 11–15

Volume 132
The Ten Practice Modules of ACI

Group 5
Advanced Books of the Asian Classics Institute
(all translated compilations from ancient classics)

Volume 54
ACI Advanced Book 1
The Path to Bliss, Part One

Volume 55
ACI Advanced Book 2
The Path to Bliss, Part Two

Volume 56
ACI Advanced Book 3
The Path to Bliss, Part Three

Volume 57
ACI Advanced Book 4
*A Rite of Empowerment into the Secret Teachings
        of the Lord of Terror (Yamantaka)*

Volume 58
ACI Advanced Book 5
The Commitments of the Secret Word

Volume 59
ACI Advanced Book 6
An Overview of the Diamond Way

Volume 60
ACI Advanced Book 7
The Blessing of the Diamond Angel (Vajra Yogini)

Volume 61
ACI Advanced Book 8
Sadhana: Reaching the Angel

Volume 62
ACI Advanced Book 9
The Yoga of the Lama, Part 1

Volume 63
ACI Advanced Book 10
The Yoga of the Lama, Part 2

Volume 64
ACI Advanced Book 11
The Yoga of the Mantra

Volume 65
ACI Advanced Book 12
Lerung: The Art of Diamond Retreat

Volume 66
ACI Advanced Book 13
A Bridge to the Stage of Completion

Volume 67
ACI Advanced Book 14
The Six Yogas of Naropa, Part 1

Volume 68
ACI Advanced Book 15
The Six Yogas of Naropa, Part 2

Volume 69
ACI Advanced Book 16
Continuing with the Stage of Completion

Volume 70
ACI Advanced Book 17
Practice with a Spiritual Partner

Volume 71
ACI Advanced Book 18

The Offering to Lamas

Volume 73
ACI Advanced Book 19
The Complete Practices of the Medicine Buddha

Group 6
Translations of Ancient Asian Classics

Volume 72
Sunlight on the Path to Freedom:
> *A Commentary to the Diamond Cutter Sutra**
> by Choney Lama Drakpa Shedrup
> (1675–1748)

Volume 74
The Principal Teachings of Buddhism*
> by Je Tsongkapa (1357–1419),
> including a commentary by Pabongka
Rinpoche (1878–1941)

Volume 75
Door to the Diamond Way*
> by Je Tsongkapa (1357–1419),
> including a commentary by Pabongka
> Rinpoche (1878–1941)

Volume 76
Poems from the Tantric College
> by Lobsang Chukyi Gyeltsen,
> His Holiness the First Panchen Lama
> (1565–1662)

Volume 77
A Door to Emptiness: The Crucial Teaching for
> *Touching the Diamond World**
> by Ngawang Tashi, of the Clan of Sey

(1678–1738)

Volume 78
The Golden Key: Difficult Questions
in the Mind Only School of Buddhism,
Part One*
original text by Je Tsongkapa (1357–1419)
commentary by Fearless Blade,
Jikme Rikpay Reldri (fl. 1775)

Volume 79
Three Treasures: A Buddhist Prayer Book
by Dakpo Lama Jampel Hlundrup Gyatso
(1845–1919),
Je Tsongkapa (1357–1419), Gyuchen
Sangye Gyatso (b. 1550),
& His Holiness the First Panchen Lama
(1565–1662)

Volume 80
Sky Flowers & Magic Shows: The Interaction of Reality
by Master Yuance of the Tang Dynasty
(613–696ᴀᴅ)
Book 1 of the Xuanzang's Legacy Series

Volume 81
Neither One nor Many: The Nature & Function of
Ultimate Reality
by Master Yuance of the Tang Dynasty
(613–696ᴀᴅ)
Book 2 of the Xuanzang's Legacy Series

Volume 82
The String of Precious Jewels: A Brief Word-by-Word
Commentary on Je Tsongkapa's "Essence of
the Ocean of Discipline"
by Je Tsongkapa (1357–1419),
including a commentary by

Gyal Kenpo Drakpa Gyeltsen (1762–1837)

Volume 83
The Sun which Illuminates the True Thought
of All the Able Ones and their Children:
A Commentary to the "Treasure House of
Higher Knowledge"
by Master Vasubandhu (350AD),
with a commentary by
Choney Lama Drakpa Shedrup
(1675–1748)

Volume 84
All Paths Are One: The Role of Understanding in
Achieving Goals
by Master Yuance of the Tang Dynasty
(613–696AD)
Book 3 of the Xuanzang's Legacy Series

Volume 85
Stopping the Circle of Sadness:
*The Buddhist Teaching of the Wheel of Life**
by Kedrup Tenpa Dargye (1493–1568)

Volume 86
Emptiness Meditations:
*Learning How to See That Nothing is Itself**
by Choney Lama, Drakpa Shedrup
(1675–1748),
with additional instruction from:
Arya Nagarjuna (200AD)
Master Kamalashila (775AD)
Pabongka Rinpoche (1878–1941)
Trijang Rinpoche (1901–1981)

Volume 87
Nothing is the Way It Seems:
*The 60 Verses of Nagarjuna**

by Master Nagarjuna (200AD), with a
commentary by Gyaltsab Je,
Darma Rinchen (1364–1432)

Volume 88
*Great Ideas of the East: A Survey of 101 Enlightening
Belief Systems from Ancient Asia**
by Choney Lama Drakpa Shedrup
(1675–1748)

Volume 89
Sunlight on Suchness: The Meaning of the Heart Sutra*
by Choney Lama Drakpa Shedrup
(1675–1748)

Volume 90
*An Expanded Commentary to "Difficult Points on
the Subject of the Negative Mind and
Foundation Consciousness"*
original text & autocommentary
by Je Tsongkapa (1357–1419)

Volume 91
*Deathless Nectar for Helping Others:
A Commentary to the "Crown of Knives"*
by Dharma Rakshita (c. 1000AD) &
Tenpa Rabgye, Throneholder of Radreng
(1759–1816)

Volume 92
The Puddle & The Sea: The Art of Interpretation
by Master Yuance of the Tang Dynasty
(613–696AD)
Book 4 of the Xuanzang's Legacy Series

Volume 93
All the Kinds of Karma*
by Lord Buddha (500BC)

Volume 94
*The Six Flavors of Emptiness: New Ways of Looking at
        Our World*
        Compilation of ancient authors

Volume 95
*A Car is Not a Car: A Commentary to the Chinese
        Edition of the "Questions of King Milinda"*
        translation of the ancient Chinese of a
        philosophical conversation between the
        Greek king Menander (140BC)
        and the Buddhist monk Nagasena,
        with a commentary compiled from
        traditional sources dating from the 14th to
        17th centuries

Volume 96
*The Source and Stopping of Pain:
        An Ancient Teaching on the Wheel of Life*
        by Master Vasubandhu (350AD)

Volume 97
*Did the Buddha Contradict Himself?
        A Study of Literal & Figurative Meaning*
        by Master Yuance of the Tang Dynasty
        (613–696AD)
        Book 5 of the Xuanzang's Legacy Series

Volume 98
*Using Contemplation to Understand How the World
        Really Works*
        by Master Yuance of the Tang Dynasty
        (613–696AD)
        Book 6 of the Xuanzang's Legacy Series

Volume 99
*Preparing for the Diamond Way: The Mountain of
        Blessings*

by Je Tsongkapa (1357–1419),
with a commentary by
Pabongka Rinpoche (1878–1941)

Volume 100
*The Three Turnings of the Wheel: The Interpretation of
Historical Periods*
by Master Yuance of the Tang Dynasty
(613–696AD)
Book 7 of the Xuanzang's Legacy Series

Volume 101
The Hidden Workings of the World
by Master Yuance of the Tang Dynasty
(613–696AD)
Book 8 of the Xuanzang's Legacy Series

Volume 102
*Destroying the Darkness in Our Minds:
An Explanation of the Seven Books of
Reasoning*
by Kedrup Je Gelek Pel Sangpo
(1385–1438)

Volume 103
*Opening the Eyes of the Fortunate: An Interlude on
Emptiness*
by Kedrup Je Gelek Pel Sangpo
(1385–1438)

Volume 104
A Gift of Liberation, Thrust into Our Hands
by Pabongka Rinpoche (1878–1941)

Volume 105
An Overview of the Middle Way
by Kedrup Tenpa Dargye (1493–1568)

Volume 106
A Dialectic Analysis of the Perfection of Wisdom
       by Kedrup Tenpa Dargye (1493–1568)

Volume 107
The Illumination of the True Thought
       by Je Tsongkapa (1357–1419)

Volume 108
A Guide to the Bodhisattva's Way of Life
       by Master Shantideva (700AD)

Volume 109
The Great Commentary to the Diamond Cutter Sutra
       by Master Kamalashila (750AD)

Volume 110
A Ship on the Sea of Emptiness: The Wisdom of
       Nagarjuna
       by Choney Lama Drakpa Shedrup
       (1675–1748)

Volume 111
The Devil Debates An Angel
       by Lobsang Chukyi Gyeltsen,
       His Holiness the First Panchen Lama
       (1565–1662)

Volume 112
The Sweet Essence of the Nectar of the Angels of the
       Three Worlds
       by Pabongka Rinpoche (1878–1941)

Volume 113
The Drumsong of the Gods, which Calls Us to
       the Paradise of the Diamond Angel
       by Yangchen Druppay Dorje (1809–1887)

Volume 114
Compassion Highway:
An Explanation of the Vows of the Bodhisattva
by Je Tsongkapa (1357–1419)

Volume 115
Changkya's Schools of Philosophy
by Changkya Rolpay Dorje (1717–1786)

Volume 116
A Gemstone of the True Intent:
A Commentary on The String of Precious Jewels
by Gyalwa Gendun Drup,
His Holiness the First Dalai Lama
(1391-1474),
with a commentary by
Panchen Lodru Leksang, 9th throneholder
of Tashi Hlunpo (c. 1510)

Volume 117
The Essence of Eloquence,
on The Art of Interpretation
by Je Tsongkapa (1357–1419),
including the text of the sutra *What I Really*
Meant, by the Buddha (500BC)

Volume 118
An Elucidation of the Fifty Verses on Lamas
by Je Tsongkapa (1357–1419)

Volume 119
The Two Sutras of the Medicine Buddha*
by the Buddha (500BC)

Volume 120
Jewel of the True Thought:
A Word-by-Word Explanation
of the "Commentary on Accurate Perception"

by Geshe Yeshe Wangchuk (1928–1997)

Volume 121
The Vimalakirti Sutra
by the Buddha (500BC)

Volume 122
The Prayers of the Seven Buddhas:
*The Longer Sutra of the Medicine Buddha**
by the Buddha (500BC)

Volume 123
A Song of My Spiritual Life
by Je Tsongkapa (1357–1419),
with a commentary by
Choney Lama Drakpa Shedrup
(1675–1748)

Volume 124
Nagarjuna's String of Precious Jewels
by Arya Nagarjuna (c. 200AD),
with a commentary by
Gyaltsab Je, Darma Rinchen (1364–1432)

Volume 125
An Explanation of the Sutra on the First Principle,
and Divisions, of Interdependence
by the Buddha (500BC),
with a commentary by
Master Vasubandhu (c. 350AD)

Volume 126
The Art of Sharing: How King Shri Sena
*Shared Everything He Had with Others**
by the Buddha (500BC)

Volume 127
Orbs for the Profound:

A Commentary to the "Praise of Dependence"
by Je Tsongkapa (1357–1419),
with a commentary by
Ngulchu Dharma Bhadra (1772–1851)

Volume 128
Eloquent Words on the Essence of the Sea of Higher
Knowledge: A Commentary to the
"Compendium of Higher Knowledge"
by Arya Asanga (c. 350AD),
with a commentary by
Gyaltsab Je, Darma Rinchen (1364–1432)

Volume 129
The Ocean of Reasoning: An Explication
of "Wisdom," the Verses of the Root Text
of the Middle Way
by Arya Nagarjuna (c. 200 AD),
with a commentary by
Je Tsongkapa (1357–1419),

Volume 133
Death Meditation
by Je Tsongkapa (1357-1419)

Volume 135
Three Lam Rims
by Je Tsongkapa (1357-1419),
with commentaries by
Pabongka Rinpoche Dechen Nyingpo
(1878-1941)
and Choney Lama Drakpa Shedrup
(1675-1748)